PRAISE FOR *LOVE LIKE THAT*

"From the first vulnerable sentence, this heart-felt message from Dr. Parrott will compel you to not only be a better person, it will show you exactly how you can do just that. Incredible!"

—Dave Ramsey, #1 bestselling author and radio host

"Dr. Parrott pulls back the curtains of misconception to reveal that loving like Jesus is more possible and more doable than you may have ever imagined. This book will positively change the way you interact with everyone."

—Dr. David Jeremiah, founder and president of Turning Point and senior pastor of Shadow Mountain Community Church in El Cajon, CA

"Grounded in research and biblical understanding, *Love Like That* reveals the Jesus-model of loving relationships in clear and practical terms. If you're like me, you will be so glad you read this book."

—Judah Smith, bestselling author of *Jesus Is _____*

"Refreshingly honest and incredibly practical. This book is for everyone who wants to love like Jesus but never thought they could. I've personally benefited from this helpful book and you will too."

—Lysa TerKeurst, president of Proverbs 31 Ministries and bestselling author of *Uninvited*

"With an incredible blend of contemporary social science and a deep understanding of Scripture, Les Parrott's writing will help you see beyond what you may be tempted to settle for. And he'll show you the way, step-by-step, to realizing the kinds of relationships we all long for."

—Lee Strobel, *New York Times* bestselling author

"I love this book. Every chapter is like a stepping stone that will bring you closer to loving like Jesus. Don't miss out on Dr. Parrott's message in *Love Like That*. It will truly transform your relationships."

—Christine Caine, founder of A21 and Propel Women

"*Love Like That* will transform the way you relate to the people in your life. Drawing on biblical wisdom and his expertise as a gifted counselor, Dr. Les Parrott provides a relational road map for reflecting the love of Jesus in every interaction you have with other people. Deeply encouraging and incredibly practical, this book will inspire you to love others the way Jesus loves you."

—Chris Hodges, senior pastor of Church of the Highlands
and author of *Fresh Air* and *The Daniel Dilemma*

"Les Parrott has provided every Christ-follower with an amazing gift—a practical road map for walking in the footsteps of Jesus. This book will revolutionize your relationships."

—Mark Batterson, *New York Times* bestselling author of *The Circle Maker* and lead pastor of National Community Church

"Les Parrott dares to write about the most challenging love of all—the love Jesus lived. Read this book and see how this seemingly impossible feat becomes more and more obtainable."

—Josh D. McDowell, author and speaker

"If you're looking for a path to be the best person you can be—to loving the people in your life like you never have before—you've got to read *Love Like That*. It's life changing."

—Chad Veach, lead pastor of Zoe Church in Los Angeles, CA

"Who should read this book? Everyone who wants better, healthier, and incredibly loving relationships. Period."

—Rich Wilkerson, Sr., senior pastor of Trinity Church in Miami, FL

"This incredible book gives you a practical plan—a truly doable way—for transforming your interactions with others. Your relationships will never be the same."

—Bob Goff, bestselling author of *Love Does*

"Les Parrott has made what seems nearly impossible to so many of us—loving like Jesus—more doable than ever. This book not only shows you what to do, it gives you the know-how to actually do it."

—Jefferson Bethke, bestselling author of *Jesus>Religion*

"Books, by their nature, often challenge us to think the right way, but *Love Like That* goes one step further: it calls us to *live* the right way—the way of Jesus. This is Dr. Les Parrott at his finest—mixing the best psychological research with a voluminous familiarity with Scripture to offer an inspiring and workable model to become more like Christ. Perfect for individual or group study."

—Gary Thomas, author of *Sacred Marriage* and *Sacred Pathways*

"In his new book, *Love Like That*, Dr. Parrott pulls back the curtain and shows us that loving like Jesus is not only possible, it's more doable than you might imagine. You'll get some challenging, real-life application that will truly make a difference in the way you interact with the people around you."

—Craig Groeschel, pastor of Life.Church and author of *Divine Direction*

"This is a beautiful, thoughtful, hopeful book—that we can love like Jesus. Loving boldly, loving wisely is not only our deepest desire, it's within our reach! I want to now more than ever!"

—John Eldridge, bestselling author of *Wild at Heart*

"We all would benefit significantly from loving more like Jesus, and in his new book, *Love Like That*, Les Parrott does an excellent job of teaching us how. I found his book both insightful and convicting, especially in our current culture. If we were all to treat others as he describes—more mindfully, approachably, graciously, boldly, and empathetically—not only would we see a transformation in our own lives and relationships, but I'm convinced we would also witness spiritual awakening in our communities. We need to get back to relating to others and communicating the message of the gospel with such awesome, biblical, Christ-empowered love."

—Dr. Charles Stanley, senior pastor of First Baptist Church Atlanta and founder and president of In Touch Ministries

LOVE LIKE THAT

ALSO BY LES PARROTT

LOVE LIKE THAT

5 Relationship Secrets from Jesus

LES PARROTT

NELSON
BOOKS

An Imprint of Thomas Nelson

Published in Nashville, Tennessee, by Nelson Books, an imprint of Thomas Nelson. Nelson Books and Thomas Nelson are registered trademarks of HarperCollins Christian Publishing, Inc.

Published in association with Yates & Yates, www.yates2.com.

Thomas Nelson titles may be purchased in bulk for educational, business, fund-raising, or sales promotional use. For information, please email SpecialMarkets@ThomasNelson.com.

ISBN 978-1-4002-0781-7 (HC)
ISBN 978-1-4002-0782-4 (eBook)
ISBN 978-1-4002-0884-5 (IE)

Library of Congress Control Number: 2018932498

Printed in the United States of America

18 19 20 21 22 LSC 10 9 8 7 6 5 4 3 2 1

For John and Jackson.
Two boys who have inspired me
to "love like that" with all my heart.
I'm in awe of your dedication to follow Jesus
and I love you more than you'll ever know.

Observe how Christ loved us. His love was not cautious but extravagant. He didn't love in order to get something from us but to give everything of himself to us. Love like that.

—Ephesians 5:2

CONTENTS

LOVE LIKE JESUS?

Love one another the way I loved you.
This is the very best way to love.

—Jesus

I'm not a softhearted poet. I'm not a people-pleasing idealist. I live with full-throttle ambition and no shortage of self-interest. I'm impatient and sometimes insecure. I jockey for position and I like exclusive privileges. I can be judgmental, insensitive, petty, and resentful. Oh, and I can be cheap and stingy.

But I want to love like Jesus.

Why? Because I know it's the best way to live. When we love like Jesus, we are lifted outside ourselves. We shed self-interest. We become less judgmental. His brand of love sees beyond the normal range of human vision—over walls of resentment and barriers of betrayal. When we love like Jesus, we rise above petty demands and snobbish entitlement. We loosen our tight-fisted anxiety and relax in a surplus of benevolence.

Most of all, the Jesus model of love inspires our spirit to transcend who we are tempted to settle for in ourselves and our relationships. It ensures that we are following the best way to live, "the most excellent way."

I want to love like that.

Getting Real

But can anyone *really* love like Jesus? After all, he raised the bar of love to extraordinary heights. Love your enemies? Walk the extra mile? Turn the other cheek? Seriously? This is love beyond reason, isn't it?

Of course.

And that's the point. Divine love defies explanation. It aims straight at the heart. And, as I'm about to show you, that's where we find its empowering secret. But let's not be too quick to dismiss our cognitive capacity when it comes to extraordinary love.

We've all heard how even the most advanced super-computers don't hold a candle to the human brain. A computer comparable to the human brain, for example, would need to be able to perform more than 38 thousand trillion operations per second. Our brains make computers look like Tinkertoys.

To say the human brain is amazing is simply an understatement. Complete understanding of the brain will be a long time coming. But truth be told, the human brain is child's play compared to the intangible human mind. "The mind is its own place," said English poet John Milton, "and in it self / Can make Heav'n of Hell, and a Hell of Heav'n." Scientists have pretty well mapped out the terrain of the brain, but they are far from understanding the complexities of the mind.

For starters, you can't x-ray the mind. It's beyond physical location. The French philosopher René Descartes declared that the mind, while it might live in the brain, was a nonmaterial thing, entirely separate from the physical tissues found inside the head. Furthermore, said Descartes, in one of history's most memorable sound bites, "I think, therefore I am." His point: consciousness is the only sure evidence that we actually exist. The Bible actually said it first: "For as he thinks in his heart, so is he." Pardon the pun, but the mind is pretty heady. It leaves scientists and philosophers alike with much to ponder.

What scientists *do* know about the mind is that it is an intensely private part of each individual. Nobody has access to its intuitive and rational parts but the owner. No one can "know your mind" unless you tell them. Your mind holds your sense of self. Your mind is synonymous with your thoughts. Thus, we "make up our minds," we "change our minds," or we are sometimes "of two minds." In fact, it's sometimes said that the mind is what your brain does. Your mind, in a word, thinks.

Here's the good news: Loving like Jesus doesn't require us to put our minds in neutral and set aside our skepticism or critical thinking. It certainly doesn't ask that we put our intellect in abeyance. Far from it. As Oswald Chambers said, "Christian thinking is a rare and difficult thing; so many seem unaware that the first great commandment according to our Lord is, 'Thou shalt love the Lord thy God . . . with all thy mind.'"

So, when it comes to the seemingly irrational ways Jesus loved others, we need to be honest, discerning, analytical, and reasoned. We need to acknowledge that it simply doesn't make sense.

Well, not quite. Truth is, it doesn't make sense if we *only* use our mind.

The Heart of the Matter

As you are reading the words on this page, your brain is sending electrical impulses through a network of brain cells so small that thousands of them could fit into the period at the end of this sentence. But these impulses are not exclusive to the brain. The heart, as it turns out, is essential to our reasoning.

Until the 1990s, scientists assumed that only the brain sent information to the heart, but now we know that it works both ways. The heart physically communicates with the brain through a complex nervous system of neurons, neurotransmitters, proteins, and other support cells. In fact, the pulse created by the heart is actually like a "blood pressure wave" that reaches and energizes every cell of the brain, influencing emotions and other activities such as attention, perception, memory, and problem-solving.

This is why expressions such as "my heart aches," "open your heart," or "my heart goes out to you" are often more than symbolic. They make a deeper connection than our rational thinking. They resonate more deeply than our thoughts.

Intelligence alone, without involvement of the heart, can be dangerous. We run the risk of becoming "heartless" or having a heart of stone. It's what Antoine de Saint-Exupéry was getting at when he said, "But eyes are blind. You have to look with the heart."

Without the heart, we lack true understanding. Without the heart, we lack the capacity to love like Jesus.

Here's the point: If we seek this high-level love

exclusively with our minds, without tuning into our heart, loving like Jesus becomes an overwhelming obligation. If we try solely to reason our way to loving like Jesus, discouragement prevails. Spiritual burnout runs rampant. If we try to love like Jesus only using our head and not our heart, Jesus becomes a mere model to follow. Love becomes a to-do list.

Now that's not all bad. But Jesus is more than a model. Jesus is a power to embrace. When we embrace the love of Jesus with our heart, when we open ourselves to accept his love again and again, we find the secret to loving like Jesus. The moment we open our heart to communicate with our head, love becomes less of an obligation and more of an empowering force. And our relationships reap the dividends.

So, to love like Jesus, we need to think *and* feel. We need reason *and* emotion. We need both our head *and* heart, working together. It's the only way to bring perfect love into our imperfect life.

Here's the bottom line: when you open your heart, love changes your mind. Let that sentence soak in. Your mind can do an about-face when it receives a divine impulse from your heart. Your mind can be transformed when it "listens" to your heart. You'll experience a revolution in your thinking when you allow your heart to enter the conversation. It's what Paul was getting at when he said, "You'll be changed from the inside out."

If you are just looking for a reasonable love, you'll miss out on an extraordinary love. You will miss out on the power to find a love you didn't know you could experience.

A Fellow Struggler

I want to love like Jesus—and so do you. You wouldn't have picked up this book if you didn't. You and I both know that loving like Jesus is the best way to live. And because of that we share a connection.

If you and I were to sit down at your kitchen table and I were to ask you why you picked up this book, I imagine that within minutes, if you felt safe, you'd tell me about your challenge to be loving with the people in your life—family, friends, coworkers, and even strangers. That's when I'd breathe a deep sigh of relief, knowing that you're my kind of person. I can identify with you.

Unfortunately, a book is a one-way conversation. So, let me answer a couple of questions I would imagine you're asking right at the start. First, why did I write this book?

I've been on a long quest, truly for decades. I've wanted to know how the ideal model of love could rub off on my imperfect life. How can self-giving love work its way into the tissues of my self-interested life? My quest has yielded answers and I feel compelled to share them. I've written this book for everyone who feels like a failure when it comes to loving like Jesus but still keeps trying.

You might also be asking what gives me the authority to write a book on such an aspirational topic. Well, you need to know that I'm not writing as a theologian or pastor—though, in full disclosure, I have an advanced degree in theology. I'm not writing as a biblical scholar who knows everything about the life of Jesus—though I've traveled to Israel and walked where Jesus walked. I'm not even writing as a social scientist—though I'm a psychologist, a researcher, a professor.

Nope. I'm writing primarily as a struggler who too often feels like a failure as I stumble, again and again, in walking in the footsteps of Jesus. I don't have a lock on it. I haven't cracked an ancient or mysterious code. But my heartfelt quest has led me to a message that I want to share with you. That's why I wrote this book.

My Hope for You

One of my biggest concerns in writing this book is that you might feel that loving like Jesus means becoming a doormat. A weak wimp. It's a common misperception.

And it's not true. Nor is it true that when you love like Jesus you miss out on all the fun. Some people think that loving like Jesus means sacrificing happiness. They think it's all about self-denial. They think it will squash joy. They are wrong.

God designed us to have a driving desire for happiness. It's bred in our bones. It's in our DNA. God wants us happy. But too often what we think will make us happy, what will give us abiding joy, won't. In fact, the great hindrance to true enjoyment is our willingness to settle for pitiful pleasures. We become accustomed to such meager, short-lived pleasures that we miss out on the deepest enjoyment of all.

It's a fundamental psychological law: when you help other people, you immediately receive a payoff yourself. Ralph Waldo Emerson is rumored to have said: "You cannot sincerely help another without helping yourself." And he could not have been more right. When we empty ourselves of our self-centered desires, when we surrender our desire to get our way, we are filled with grace. Each act of kindness improves our relationships. Each act of self-giving love expands our life.

Numerous studies find that the ability to practice appreciation and love is the *defining* mark of the happiest of human beings. When people engage in self-giving love by doing something extraordinarily positive, they use higher-level brain functions and set off a series of neurochemical reactions that shower their system in positive emotions.

Perhaps you are wondering if this kind of happiness is triggered just as readily by having fun as it is by an act of self-giving love. Martin Seligman, of the University of Pennsylvania, wondered the same thing. He gave his students an assignment: to engage in one pleasurable activity and one philanthropic activity and then to write about both. Turns out, the "pleasurable" activity of hanging out with friends, watching a movie, or eating a delicious dessert paled in comparison with the effects of the loving action. Seligman stated that "when our philanthropic acts were spontaneous . . . the whole day went better." He went on to say that self-giving love is not accompanied by a separable stream of positive emotion; rather "it consists in total engagement and in the loss of self-consciousness." Time stops when we lend a helping hand, nurture a hurting soul, or offer a listening ear.

No one has ever developed into a well-rounded personality, or has lived an effective life, unless he has learned to love others without selfish gain. This single skill is the very hinge upon which happy living hangs. Without a generous spirit, a benevolent attitude, and a civilized mind-set, a person's life remains in the dark ages.

Let me say it straight: Until you wrap your life in love—the kind Jesus modeled—you will never be genuinely happy. Fulfillment forever eludes us if we do not honor the law of love. So my hope for you in reading this book is that you would tap into the deepest and most abiding source of joy on the planet: loving like Jesus. Each of the five chapters reveals little-known actions Jesus gave us for doing just that. I call them "secrets" because they are relatively unknown. They operate under wraps. Most people most of the time are not aware of just how doable these loving practices are because we equate the whole idea of loving like Jesus solely to sacrifice. Or we chalk these loving behaviors up to saint-like acts reserved exclusively for those who live a near-monastic or cloistered life. That's a mistake.

Loving like Jesus can be a daily reality for anyone who chooses it. The five chapters of this book are practical everyday behaviors that don't require you to give up on fun. I want to say it again: Loving like Jesus does not mean becoming a miserable namby-pamby or monkish doormat. Loving like Jesus is the ultimate secret to enjoying fulfilling relationships.

My Promise to You

I also want you to know—right at the top—that I'm optimistic about you and me. I believe we can both become better at loving like Jesus. Why? Because this love isn't elusive. It isn't pie-in-the-sky. It isn't out of reach or relegated to untouchable saints. It's real. Jesus gives us practical examples of how to love in extraordinary ways. And you're likely closer to it than you know.

Surprised? Me too. And relieved. Why? Because Jesus wasn't a softhearted people pleaser. He most certainly didn't try to make everyone happy. He wasn't always "nice." He got frustrated in his relationships. And he didn't continually bury his own desires to project a smug or sanctimonious superiority.

Loving more like Jesus is more obtainable than you might imagine. His teaching and example reveal at least five distinct qualities of his love:

When you love like Jesus,

- you become more *mindful*—less detached.
- you become more *approachable*—less exclusive.
- you become more *grace-full*—less judgmental.
- you become more *bold*—less fearful.
- you become more *self-giving*—less self-absorbed.

Is this an exhaustive list of how Jesus loved? Of course not. But it's a way to get an earthly handle on this heavenly ideal. Time and again, Jesus demonstrated these five qualities and spoke about them, but not as unreachable ideals. He calls us to embody them.

Are they difficult? You bet. But not insurmountable. Will you and I fail in living them out? Absolutely. But don't be discouraged. For it's in our failed attempts that we learn to better reason with our hearts as well as our heads.

I'll be honest. I feel a little like the Tin Woodman in *The Wonderful Wizard of Oz* who said, "Once I had brains, and a heart also; so, having tried them both, I should much rather have a heart." Why? Truth be told, I'm inclined to lean into thinking with my head more than reasoning with my heart. But the more I follow Jesus, the more I find reasons to love by tapping into the reasoning of my heart.

So here's my pledge. You won't find pat answers or spiritual platitudes in these pages. No sanctimonious sayings or stories of false humility. You won't find the proverbial "three easy steps" or ridiculously simple "quick fixes." No philosophical mumbo jumbo or psychobabble. I'm committed to real life. I'm committed to authenticity that reveals a practical path to healthy and fulfilling relationships.

You won't find guilt or shame as a message in this book. Instead you'll find encouragement and practicality as we continue our quest to travel the most excellent way.

CHAPTER 1

MINDFUL

Don't you see the point of all this?

—Jesus

The two hundred university students in my psychology class have no idea what's about to happen. But in a few moments, they will be dumbfounded.

I'm showing them a brief video containing six basketball players—some dressed in black, some in white. The people in white have a basketball and, during the film, pass it to one another. I ask the students to watch the video and count the number of times they pass the ball.

At the end of the film, I have one simple question: "Did you spot the gorilla?"

Most students look at me blankly. You can see it on their faces: *Gorilla? Has Dr. Parrott lost his mind?* Before they have time to process my question, I show the brief film again but tell them to forget the counting—"Just watch the film this time."

I show the very same video. And the reactions are fascinating. Some are stunned into silence, slack-jawed. Some laugh uncontrollably. Some question whether I'm showing a completely different video.

But I'm not.

Halfway through the brief film, a man dressed as a gorilla slowly saunters through the players, beats his chest at the camera and then walks off. It's plain as day. How could anyone miss it?

But nearly every one of my students *does* miss it. And they aren't the only ones. The film, known as the "invisible gorilla" test, was developed by Harvard researchers Dan Simons and Christopher Chabris. They wanted to show us that we are not as attuned to our environment as much as we think we are. In fact, we often miss what's right in front of us.

The study has been replicated with countless variations since they first conducted the research in 1999. The gorilla has been replaced with everything from a moon-walking bear to a clown on a unicycle—and to unsuspecting audiences they're all just as "invisible" as the gorilla.

The eye sees only what the mind is prepared to comprehend.

—Robertson Davies

One of my favorite variations of the study involves a group of credentialed radiologists at a prestigious Boston hospital who continually fail to spot a dancing gorilla placed on a CT scan for a typical lung screening. Using eye-tracking technology, researchers could see the radiologists looking straight at the gorilla on the slide, yet only 16 percent of radiologists spotted it.

In another experiment, people who were walking across a college campus were asked by a stranger for directions. During the resulting chat, two men carrying a wooden door passed between the stranger and the subjects. After the door went by, the subjects were asked if they had noticed anything change. Half of those tested failed to notice that, as the door passed by, the stranger had been substituted with a man who was of different height, of different build, and who sounded different. He was also wearing different clothes. Despite the fact that the subjects had talked to the stranger for ten to fifteen seconds before the swap, half of them did not detect that they were now speaking to a different person.

The point of these studies is plain: we humans are astonishingly prone to missing what should be abundantly obvious. The researchers call it "perceptual blindness." We look but fail to see. Or we see without observing. In other words, because of a lack of attention, we become blind to what's going on in plain sight.

And make no mistake: we are all susceptible to this kind of "blindness"—until we become attentive. Until we become mindful.

The Mindfulness of Jesus

Jesus "saw" what others didn't. In fact, the Gospels mention that Jesus "saw" forty times. And when he "saw," he was almost always moved with compassion.

An unexpected encounter Jesus had while traveling to Jerusalem through Jericho is a prime example of Jesus seeing beyond the obvious. Famous for its great palm trees and balsam groves that perfumed the air for miles around, Jericho was a desirable place to live. And because this town near the Jordan River was so pleasant, it became one of the most highly taxed towns in Israel.

Of course, at the time, Israel was part of the Roman Empire, and Rome did everything it could to squeeze towns like Jericho for as much money as possible. But rather than having Romans collect the taxes, the government found a few greedy Israelites to do the collecting for them. They'd auction off an area to an unscrupulous local who would then scheme ways to collect as much tax money as possible.

These conniving tax collectors literally sold out their fellow citizens to their enemy, Rome, just to make a profit. Not surprisingly, they were despised. Nobody trusted a tax collector. Imagine the feelings you might have toward a countryman who made lots of money by becoming a spy for an enemy country or a ruthless pimp or Mafia member.

> **When he looked out over the crowds, his heart broke.**
>
> —Matthew 9:37

One of these lowlife tax collectors was a man named Zaccaeus. In fact, he was a chief tax collector, which meant he was good at collecting taxes from the rich and poor alike, and he had others working for him. It also meant he was corrupt to the core and incredibly despised. Money was his sole motive, even if it cost him everything else—friends, respect, and decency. He literally bet his life on wealth to make him happy. But it wasn't working.

That's what Jesus saw. Nobody else saw Zaccaeus the way Jesus did.

As Jesus makes his way into Jericho, a crowd grows. Zaccaeus couldn't get a good view of this man who is creating all the commotion, so he climbs up a tree. He wants to see over the crowd, and he's probably wanting to hide. A tax collector with his reputation isn't trying to be conspicuous.

But Jesus draws closer, spying someone in the tree. Looking up, with hundreds of people gathering around, Jesus says one word: "Zacchaeus." The crowd can't believe it. Neither can the tax collector. He thought he was going to watch from a safe distance, and all of a sudden Jesus is calling his name and asking him to climb down. Incredibly, Jesus wants to visit with Zacchaeus at his home. The crowd is murmuring: "Why would he want to see this traitor?" Everyone went out of their way to avoid Zacchaeus, and Jesus is initiating a house call with him!

Why? Because Jesus sees what the crowd did not. While "all who saw it," as Luke says, were repulsed by Zacchaeus, Jesus treats this crooked and broken man with dignity. Jesus sees that Zacchaeus, the man who sold his soul for money, is empty and alone. Jesus sees that Zacchaeus no longer wants to live a life of dishonesty and greed. He's done sinning against God and his own people. Zacchaeus wants to come out of hiding, pay back the people he's cheated, and follow Jesus.

It's one of the most dramatic conversion stories in the Bible. And it was the result of Jesus seeing what others didn't.

The life of Jesus is filled with these perceptive incidents. Where others saw a paralyzed man, Jesus saw faith. Where others saw a political traitor, Jesus saw a new disciple. Where others saw crowds of harassing people, Jesus saw people being harassed. Where others saw sinners, Jesus saw people in need of mercy.

How did Jesus see what others didn't? It comes down to being mindful.

Mindful

adjective
mind•ful \'mīn(d)-fəl\

What does it mean to be mindful? Quite simply, it means giving others special attention. Well, of course, right? But it's more profound than you might first guess. A person who is mindful is not detached or oblivious; they see what is not readily perceptible. A mindful person is watchful. They have their eye out for what others are missing. Mindfulness attends to details—little nonverbal behaviors that often speak more loudly than words. As the dictionary makes clear, to be attentive or mindful means to "express affectionate interest through close observation and gallant gestures."

Gallant gestures! Didn't see that coming, did you? It means that if you are to be mindful, you need to be brave. The gallant person goes where others may fear to travel. And that's exactly what Jesus did. When we are mindful, we explore uncharted territory.

It's uncharted because we don't know where it will lead. But we do know that love results whenever we take a mindful journey.

What Keeps Us from Being Mindful?

I can answer this question with one word: agendas. Everyone has an agenda. All the time. It may be to save money, save time, read a book, book a flight, buy clothes, look cool, watch the news, complete a project, make food, make a call, play a game, run an errand—the list goes on and on. There is no end to it.

Your agenda is nothing more than your immediate goal. That includes what you want to do (finish this chapter, decide on dinner plans, take a walk), what you want to feel (enlightened, challenged, superior), and what you want to talk about (a vacation, a project at work, how you felt hurt last night).

Your personal agenda is continually updated and revised. And it's a powerful force. It compels you to keep your focus on your goal. Like an executive running a high-powered board meeting, you don't want to veer away from your agenda because it means you may not reach your goal. Every moment of every day we have an agenda.

If you stop to
be kind, you
must swerve
often from
your path.

—Mary Webb

Well, almost.

We all have a personal agenda until we don't. Every one of us has the capacity to set aside our self-interest, temporarily. We have the ability at any time to press the pause button on what we want. And that's the moment we see other people who have *their* own agendas. That's the moment we become mindful. That's the moment we make room for love.

The person who is unwilling to set aside their own agenda is like a person who is wearing mirrored sunglasses with the lenses flipped around. As they look out at the world, all they can see is a reflection of their own needs and desires. It's called *egocentrism*—the well-established psychological phenomenon of not being able to recognize other people's needs. In the normal humdrum of life, it's easy to become incredibly self-absorbed. We're consumed with what we need to do or where we need to be. If we aren't intentional, it becomes second nature. We become so self-absorbed and detached from others that we only think about ourselves. Other people's needs or feelings don't cross our minds.

Here's the hard truth: Loving like Jesus is not efficient. It takes time away from our own agenda-driven pace. It can mean losing control of your schedule. It causes us to get sidetracked with another person who is not on our agenda. And that's what keeps us from being mindful. If you want to love like Jesus, you need to abandon your own agenda, if only temporarily, to see what others don't.

How Mindful Are You?

If you're curious to get a little snapshot of how inclined you currently are to practice mindfulness in order to love others well, take a moment to honestly indicate how frequently you experienced each of the following over the past week. You can complete your self-test online at LoveLikeThatBook.com and receive a summary of your progress along the way.

**I'm aware of thoughts I'm
having when my mood changes.**

Never	Rarely	Sometimes	Often	Very Often

**I ask God for wisdom to recognize needs,
thoughts, and feelings in others.**

Never	Rarely	Sometimes	Often	Very Often

**I'm intentional about sincerely
being my best self with others.**

Never	Rarely	Sometimes	Often	Very Often

**Recognizing and acknowledging what others
are thinking and feeling comes easy to me.**

| Never | Rarely | Sometimes | Often | Very Often |

**I'm very aware when someone else is feeling
embarrassed or emotionally wounded.**

| Never | Rarely | Sometimes | Often | Very Often |

I manage my emotions very well.

| Never | Rarely | Sometimes | Often | Very Often |

**I set aside my own immediate plans and goals
to help someone with their personal agenda.**

| Never | Rarely | Sometimes | Often | Very Often |

**I listen for and am attuned to God's
promptings for me in relationship to others.**

| Never | Rarely | Sometimes | Often | Very Often |

**I'm mindful of God's presence
with me—I hear his whispers.**

| Never | Rarely | Sometimes | Often | Very Often |

**I'm good at relaxing my own busy agenda
in order to tune into someone else's.**

| Never | Rarely | Sometimes | Often | Very Often |

Now take a moment to review these items. If most of your answers are "often" and "very often," you're well on your way to being mindful. Your disposition to willingly set aside your own agenda is strong and will serve you well. If, on the other hand, most of your answers are "never" and "rarely," you will benefit significantly from Jesus' teaching on being mindful. In fact, you are in a prime place to see the proverbial needle move toward positive change in your capacity to set your own agenda aside to see what others don't.

What Jesus Taught Us
About Being Mindful

By all accounts, Jesus was a masterful teacher. One of his favorite ways to teach was through a story or parable. The Gospels recount nearly fifty different parables from Jesus, each of them simple, memorable, and profound.

Consider the good Samaritan, one of the most popular parables. The very phrase "good Samaritan" has been enshrined in our culture by its use in the names of hospitals and care centers worldwide. It's a story that's told and retold in classes and sermons every week. It is one of those passages, like the Christmas and Easter stories, which probably wear out professional preachers because its point seems obvious: be kind to those who are down on their luck.

> **Readily recognize what he wants from you, and quickly respond to it.**
>
> —Romans 12:1

But once you understand the background of this well-known teaching from Jesus, its lesson becomes far more profound. The original impact of the parable is lost without understanding its context. Today the positive figure of the Samaritan is almost a cultural given. But when Jesus gave this lesson, a Samaritan would have been the exact opposite, a notorious bad guy. He's the last person you'd expect to be hailed as a positive example.

Jesus' target audience for his teaching, the Jews, hated Samaritans. They regarded Samaritans as the worst of the worst, in part because they violated Jewish law by worshipping idols and they harbored criminals and outlaws. So how could Jesus set up a Samaritan as the hero of this story? From the Jewish perspective, it's a bit like Jesus telling a modern-day story involving a "good Nazi." How could he expect to win over his audience?

But he does.

You already know what happens in this dramatic tale of a roadside mugging, but let me remind you. "A man was going down from Jerusalem to Jericho," Jesus said, "and he fell among robbers, who stripped him and beat him, and departed, leaving him half dead." Everyone who was listening knew about the seventeen-mile Jericho Road that led to Jerusalem. It was lined with caves that made good hideouts for desperadoes.

Jesus goes on to describe how a priest, a pillar of the community with a personal agenda driving him to the temple, quickly walked by the beaten man, apparently giving the man in need no notice whatsoever.

Then Jesus introduces a second-level priest, still an expert in the Jewish law, known as a Levite. He definitely sees the man in pain, giving him a good look, but keeps walking.

> **"The eye is the lamp of the body."**
>
> —Jesus

Then a jarring plot twist. A villain, a person from Samaria, comes along. He's the one least likely to show compassion for the man. But he did. He sees this man in dire need of help, and he goes above and beyond what anyone would expect. He dresses the man's wounds with wine (to disinfect) and oil (to soothe the pain). He puts the man on his animal and takes him to an inn for a time of healing. And the Samaritan pays the innkeeper with his own money.

In historical context, it's easy to see that Jesus' parable is about more than helping someone in need. He is saying, "Open your eyes, and see what even the most religious and most devout are missing right in front of them." He's saying that even if your personal agenda seems holy and righteous, you may need to set it aside if you are to be loving.

Jesus is teaching us about being mindful.

Princeton University psychologists John Darley and Daniel Batson conducted a landmark study years ago that is now recounted in nearly every university course on social psychology. I want you to know about it. Here's what happened: The researchers met with a group of seminarians individually and asked each to prepare a short extemporaneous talk, then walk over to a nearby building on the campus to present it. Along the way to give their talk, each student ran into a man set up by the researchers, an actor. He was in obvious need of help, slumped over, head down, eyes closed, coughing and groaning. The question was, who would stop and lend a hand?

To highlight the results, Darley and Batson introduced some variables. For example, they varied the topic the students were to talk on. Some were asked to speak on their vocation as a member of the clergy. Others were given the parable of the good Samaritan. Also, for some students, the experimenter would look at his watch and say, "Oh, you're late. They were expecting you a few minutes ago. We'd better get moving." In other cases, he would say, "It will be a few minutes before they're ready for you, but you might as well head over now."

Which of these seminary students do you think was most likely to stop to help the man in need? If you're like almost everyone else, you'd say that those who had just read the parable of the good Samaritan would be the most likely to stop and help. Almost everyone says that. But they are wrong.

In fact, having just read the story of Jesus' teaching made almost no difference. "It is hard to think of a context in which norms concerning helping those in distress are more salient than for a person thinking about the Good Samaritan, and yet it did not significantly increase helping behavior," Darley and Batson concluded. "Indeed, on several occasions, a seminary student going to give his talk on the parable of the Good Samaritan literally stepped over the victim as he hurried on his way."

We all struggle to set aside self-interest and let go of our personal agenda. Pride, not to mention our schedule—our agenda—seems to continually interfere with our loving efforts. No wonder Jesus relayed the story of the good Samaritan.

How to Be More Mindful

So what about you? Whom do you identify with most in Jesus' story? I have to admit that my agenda-driven nature would most likely look the other way. I cringe at the thought that I might actually step over a person in pain to get where I'm going. But in all honesty, that just might be me.

At least it's me until I put my self-focus in abeyance to see what's blatantly obvious. It's me until I set aside my own agenda to become less self-absorbed. It's me until I clear my head enough to be mindful. It's me until I quiet my spirit enough to hear God whisper.

Albert Einstein called it "the sacred gift." He was commenting on the spiritual implications of listening to God's "still small voice." Einstein, one of the greatest scientific minds in history, pondered how unreasoned, intuitive moments just might be heavenly whispers. Could it be?

Here's what we know from science. If God is on your mind, if you think about relating to God over time and learning to love like Jesus, your brain makes some surprising changes. Literally. Neural functioning actually begins to alter. It turns out that being "transformed by the renewing of your mind" is more than metaphorical. Neurological renewal occurs when we focus on God. Different circuits become activated, while others

There's far more here than meets the eye. The things we see now are here today, gone tomorrow. But the things we can't see now will last forever.

—2 Corinthians 4:18

become deactivated. New dendrites are formed, new synaptic connections are made, and the brain becomes more sensitive to subtle realms of experience. That's right—the more you relate to God, the more you focus on loving like Jesus, the more your brain becomes attuned to hearing that "still small voice."

But here's the hitch. You've got to relax the tension around your busy agenda to make room for subtle and intuitive promptings of God's Spirit. The word *intuition* comes from the Latin word *intueri*, which is roughly translated as meaning "to contemplate." Our intuition stems from what we are considering, what we are attuned to. So if you want to hear from God, you've got to be attuned to his Spirit. That's when the sacred gift of God's whispers is heard.

If you're not attuned to God or mindful of his presence, you miss out on the sacred gift. John, the author of several biblical writings, puts it bluntly: "Whoever belongs to God hears what God says. The reason you do not hear is that you do not belong to God." It's echoed many times throughout the pages of the Bible: "Whoever is united with the Lord is one with him in spirit."

A recent survey of over twenty thousand Christians between the ages of fifteen and eighty-eight found that busyness is the greatest challenge we face in being mindful of God. Sixty percent say that it's "often" or "always" true that "the busyness of life gets in the way of developing my relationship with God." And when it's just pastors who are asked the question, it bumps up to 65 percent.

So what can we do? How can we calm the chaos and complexity in our hurried heads and self-consuming agendas? The answer is actually quite simple. It's found in this short sentence: "Be still, and know that I am God."

I can almost hear you asking: "How in the world can I be still when life is so fast?" It's a fair question.

God does not expect us to be contemplative monks in order to hear his voice and love like Jesus. He merely asks that we be attuned to his presence—even in the calamity and chaos of our lives. Being still does not necessarily mean retreating to a quiet place. It means quieting our minds, even in the midst of chaos, by not striving so hard. It means putting our minds at ease and letting God be God. It means seeing what others don't.

> **Once they saw, they understood.**
>
> —Mother Teresa

"We may ignore, but we can nowhere evade, the presence of God," said C. S. Lewis. "The world is crowded with Him. He walks everywhere *incognito*." Lewis, of course, did not mean that it's a game of trying to figure out where God is. Quite the contrary. God is everywhere, even in the most common of places, when we become mindful enough to notice. Our agendas, with deadlines, worries, tasks, and drives, keep us looking down. They force us to focus, almost exclusively, on our own story. Our personal agendas prevent us from looking up to see the bigger story. And the bigger story, the story of all stories, is that we are missing out on opportunities to love like Jesus.

"Earth's crammed with heaven, / And every common bush afire with God," said Elizabeth Barrett Browning. "But only he who sees, takes off his shoes; / The rest sit round it, and pluck blackberries." Don't you feel that you're sometimes missing out on God's voice, on opportunities to love like Jesus, because you aren't attuned to the holy ground you're walking on? Oblivious to what God could have done—or what Jesus would have seen—we miss the spectacular signs of his promptings because we're overly focused on the details of our own agenda.

Try this. While your mind is consumed with the clutter of your ever-changing agenda, ask God for wisdom. Sounds too simple, I know. But I urge you to ask. In fact, ask boldly without a second thought. And make it a habit. The invitation is as clear as day: "If any of you lacks wisdom, you should ask God, who gives generously."

When you still your mind enough to sense God, you begin to see what others don't. You get wise to God's promptings. Did you know the English word *wisdom* is derived from an old Anglo-Saxon word meaning "to see"? And in Greek it means "clear." Wisdom is what enables us to see the big picture clearly. It enables us to become proficient at hearing God's whispers. Wisdom enables us to take off our proverbial shoes as we cross holy ground and learn to love like Jesus.

To Ponder

- Do you agree that we humans can often be astonishingly prone to missing what should be abundantly obvious? Why or why not? Can you identify a specific time when you were "perceptually blind" to something in plain sight?
- How do you relate to Zacchaeus? What kinds of feelings would you have had toward him if you were standing nearby and observing Jesus wanting to visit with this man so many despised? How would you have felt in the moment? Why?
- How does your personal agenda—your immediate goal—keep you from recognizing other people's needs around you? Are you motivated to be more mindful of your own agenda to better love others?

Attention is
so valuable
we don't just
give it, we pay
attention. It's
like money.

—John Ortberg

- In reading about Jesus' teaching on the good Samaritan, can you imagine what you would have been thinking if you were there, in person, listing to these words? How would you have processed this idea of what we might call a "good Nazi" today?

- How would you rate your current capacity to set your own agenda aside to more clearly see other people and ways to better love them? Are you now more inclined to ask God for wisdom in doing just that? Why or why not?

CHAPTER 2

APPROACHABLE

Walk with me.

—Jesus

I felt left out. Snubbed. I was one of three speakers who had just stepped off the platform of a hotel ballroom filled with over a thousand people who seemed to appreciate my remarks. I was feeling good. I assumed I'd be going to dinner with the other two speakers to debrief and relax. But they had other plans—and I wasn't a part of them.

Big deal, right? It's trivial, really. Then why do I still remember it years later? I wince at the idea that such a minor and incidental event is still even in my memory bank. Surely I'm not that sensitive. Or am I?

Turns out we humans are highly sensitive to feeling ignored. We have an innate desire to be welcomed, and it stings when we're not included. Researchers at Purdue University use a surprisingly simple strategy called Cyberball to demonstrate just how attuned we are to feeling left out. A subject plays an online game of catch with two other players. Eventually the two other players begin throwing the ball only to each other, excluding the subject. That's it. The whole process takes less than a couple of minutes.

But here's the question: Could such a seemingly innocuous experience make any emotional difference? Could being left out of a simple game of catch by two fictitious online players be of any personal consequence? The answer, surprisingly, is yes. In fact, the same two regions of our brain that become active when we are suffering physical pain become active when we're excluded from a simple game on the computer. Imagine how our suffering is compounded in real-world rejection—with actual people.

Psychologists call our needs to be included our *affiliative drive*. Social scientists call our longing for belonging *assimilation* or *social webbing*. Others call it *fellowship* or *connecting*. Whatever it's called, everyone agrees that we're born with an insatiable inner need to be included. And make no mistake: no one is too big, strong, talented, or tough to not feel left out.

Pride is our greatest enemy and humility our greatest friend.

—John R. W. Stott

In fact, we'll go to great lengths to not be left out. We'll even sacrifice our own sensibilities. Imagine yourself in the following situation: You and seven others arrive to participate in an experiment and are seated at a table in a small room. You don't know it at the time, but the others are actually associates of the experimenter, and their behavior has been carefully scripted. You're the only real participant.

The experimenter arrives and tells you that the study in which you are about to participate concerns people's visual judgments. She places two cards before you. The card on the left contains one vertical line. The card on the right displays three lines of varying length.

The experimenter asks all of you, one at a time, to choose which of the three lines on the right card matches the length of the line on the left card. The task is repeated several times with different cards that look like this:

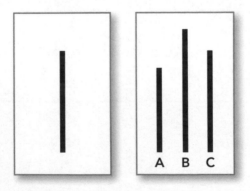

On some occasions, the other "participants" unanimously choose the wrong line just to be included. It is clear to you that they are wrong, but they have all given the same answer. What would you do? Would you go along with the majority opinion, or would you trust your own eyes?

It might surprise you to know that in this now-classic experiment, first conducted in 1951 by Solomon Asch, 75 percent of all participants in this situation go along with the rest of the group at least once. They conform. Knowing that it doesn't make sense, they agree with their peers just to be included. They don't want to be left out.

Nothing reaches so deeply into the human personality, tugs so tightly, as being included. We long to belong. Jesus understood this deep and powerful need like nobody else. It's why he was intentionally and profoundly and often shockingly approachable. In fact, Jesus was probably the most approachable person who ever lived.

The Approachability of Jesus

Jesus was tuned into outcasts, people on the fringes—those who were the most likely to feel left out or excluded. The Gospels are abundantly clear: Jesus was shockingly accessible to anyone who felt undesirable or unwanted—lepers, Gentiles, tax collectors, the poor and persecuted, pagans and sinners. He wasn't like other "holy men" in Judea. His fellow rabbis operated on the principles of exclusion and isolation. Seeing how imminently approachable Jesus was made them not just perplexed, but indignant. One of the most compelling examples occurred when Jesus was invited to dinner by a rabbi named Simon.

> **Jesus was the man for others.**
>
> —Dietrich Bonhoeffer

Jesus had preached his Sermon on the Mount just three months earlier. It drew multitudes into the rolling hills of Galilee to hear him. Perhaps Simon, a Pharisee—one who officially interprets the Jewish religious law—was in the audience that day. In his sermon, Jesus not only attempted to inspire his listeners who were feeling oppressed under Roman rule but also set forth his own interpretation of religious law, talking about adultery, lying, murder, giving to the poor, loving your enemies, praying, and, most alarming to a pious Pharisee like Simon, deferring to God even if that means defying the powers that be.

Whether or not he had been on the hillside and heard the sermon, Simon invited Jesus to dinner to discuss what Jesus was teaching. The dinner conversation would not be friendly, however. Simon was smug and wanted to trap Jesus the Nazarene into saying something blasphemous, embarrassing Jesus in front of the other dinner guests.

Simon was contemptuous before the conversation even began. Though Jesus walked the four dusty miles from Capernaum to Magdala in sandals to be there, Simon did not provide him with the customary means to wash the dust from his feet. Nor did Simon greet Jesus with a customary and respectful kiss on the cheek or anoint him with olive oil upon his arrival. It was a chilly reception, to say the least.

At the dinner, a young woman, a prostitute who has heard Jesus speak—a woman who has performed shameful acts of conformity in an attempt to be accepted—slips into the room quietly. She's been invited by Simon as part of his devious plan to test Jesus. The scene is immediately awkward. A woman with her reputation would never enter the home of a holy Pharisee, let alone be part of a dinner hosted by a Pharisee. Nevertheless, the woman stands behind Jesus at his feet (people reclined rather than sat at the dinner table in Jesus' time). She holds an expensive alabaster jar of perfume in her hands. Nobody asks how she can afford it. It's well known in the small towns of Galilee how this woman, Mary Magdalene, makes her money.

She shocks everyone when she bends down to open the fragrant perfume. She's overcome with emotion. Knowing Jesus' message of grace and forgiveness, she begins to sob. Her tears flow freely as her face is pressed to the dusty feet of Jesus. They mix with the perfume she applies to his feet.

Gaining her composure, she then does something that is never done. She lets down her hair, a violation of social custom because respectable Jewish woman always kept their hair bound in public. But she's doing this in homage, to dry the Nazarene's feet with her long hair, as she kisses them with respect.

Simon waits to see how Jesus will respond to this sinner who is doing such scandalous things. Jesus says, "Simon, I have something to tell you."

"Oh? Tell me."

"Two men were in debt to a banker. One owed five hundred silver pieces, the other fifty. Neither of them could pay up, and so the banker canceled both debts. Which of the two would be more grateful?"

Simon answered, "I suppose the one who was forgiven the most."

"That's right," said Jesus. Then turning to the woman, but speaking to Simon, he said, "Do you see this woman? I came to your home; you provided no water for my feet, but she rained tears on my feet and dried them with her hair. You gave me no greeting, but

Jesus was able
to love because
he loved right
through the
layer of mud.

—Helmut Thielicke

from the time I arrived she hasn't quit kissing my feet. You provided nothing for freshening up, but she has soothed my feet with perfume. Impressive, isn't it? She was forgiven many, many sins, and so she is very, very grateful. If the forgiveness is minimal, the gratitude is minimal."

Then Jesus spoke to her: "I forgive your sins."

That set the dinner guests talking behind his back: "Who does he think he is, forgiving sins!" He ignored them and said to the woman, "Your faith has saved you. Go in peace."

As I said, Jesus is shockingly accessible. If he excludes anyone, it's the people who are exclusive (pious religious leaders). But, in the case of Simon, he readily accepted his dinner invitation, knowing it wouldn't be pleasant. The bottom line is that Jesus made himself approachable to everyone: rich or poor, schooled or unschooled, healthy or sick.

People of his day tended to keep rabbis and "holy men" at a respectful distance, but Jesus was open-armed. People crowded around him just to touch his clothes. When Jesus called his disciples, he didn't recruit exclusive priests or rabbis. He sought out lowly laborers, fishermen, and even a disreputable tax collector (Matthew). When a group of little children were brought to see Jesus, the disciples tried to keep them away from him, believing someone as important as Jesus should not be that approachable. But Jesus was affronted, telling his disciples, "Let the little children come to me and do not hinder them." Jesus took them in his arms and blessed them. Jesus was a friend to the innocent as well as to sinners. In fact, the more unsavory the characters, the more at ease they seemed to feel around Jesus. He made sinners feel so comfortable that it often made pious people feel uncomfortable. In short, Jesus moved the emphasis from law (exclusive) to love (inclusive). Relationships, for Jesus, superseded rules.

Perhaps it was because Jesus knew so much rejection in his own life. After all, his life was *defined* by rejection. His neighbors laughed at him, his family questioned his sanity, his closest friends betrayed him, and his countrymen eventually tried him as a revolutionary. Maybe that's why Jesus was so inclusive of those who were also rejected, the riffraff fringe who were rarely included by others. Or maybe it's because Jesus, the God-man, simply had immeasurable understanding and insight into our longing for belonging. Whatever the reason, make no mistake: Jesus went out of his way to embrace the unloved and unworthy. He went out of his way to be approachable to everyone.

Approachable

adjective
ap•proach•able \ə-'prō-chə-bəl\

The Greek word for *approachable* is *parresia* and can be translated as "a plainness in speech." In other words it means *"accessible, easy to understand."* And if you look for synonyms for this word, you'll find words like friendly, open, amenable, and accessible.

But perhaps the best way of defining *approachable* is with a common smile. Studies show that people think they already know someone if that person smiles at them, even if it's an absolute stranger. Even a fleeting smile has the capacity to burrow deep into the subconscious of the person who sees it and set off positive changes from within. For example, a smile of just a mere four-thousandths of a second (what researchers refer to as *subliminal priming*) is enough to produce a mini emotional high in others; it makes people see things around them in a more positive light. Boring material becomes more interesting; a nondescript picture seems to have more flair. Indeed, researchers have found that some foods even taste better when preceded by a subliminal smile. And what's more, these expressions are contagious: in one study, when participants were exposed to these smiles—even though they couldn't remember seeing them—their own faces mirrored what they "saw."

You may think facial expressions simply reflect your feelings, but to some extent they cause them as well. In fact, studies have shown that expressions may act like the volume control: rev up your smile, and you instantly become more approachable.

What Keeps Us from Being Approachable?

A snob is a person who believes there's a correlation between social status and human worth. Snobs basically see certain people as inherently inferior to themselves based on beliefs, values, intellect, talent, wealth, education, beauty, ethnicity, religion, or just about anything.

So, are you a snob? Before you answer, keep in mind that if you look down your nose at snobs you're actually acting a bit snobbish yourself, right? Let's face it—we're all inclined to think we are superior to others in some ways some of the time. It's our nature. That's why the single biggest barrier to being more approachable is pride.

Pride is all about being exclusive, not inclusive. It's the basis for the old British joke: leave three Englishmen in a room, and they will invent a rule that prevents a fourth from joining them. It's why comedian Groucho Marx makes us smile when he sends notice to the Friars Club of Beverly Hills: "Please accept my resignation. I don't want to belong to any club that will accept people like me as a member." Pride makes a mockery of our attempts to include others, to be approachable.

The antidote to unhealthy pride is, of course, humility. And *humility*, when traced to its origin, literally means "from the earth." In other words, humility steps off its high horse to be common and lowly.

In Nikos Kazantzakis's novel *Christ Recrucified*, there is a scene in which four village men confess their sins to one another in the presence of the pope. One of the men, Michelis, cries out in bloated humility, "How can God let us live on the earth? Why doesn't he kill us to purify creation?"

"Because, Michelis," the pope answered, "God is a potter; he works in mud."

Whether you see it the same way or not, the point is that humility is lowly. And that's where God meets us—in the places where we are humble. That's where we become malleable. It's where we soften our shell and ease our ego.

Healthy pride, the pleasant emotion of being

pleased by our work, is quite different from unhealthy pride, where our ego is bloated. The latter is laced with arrogance. You don't have to be an egomaniac to suffer from unhealthy pride. It has a way of secretly seeping into the crevices of our lives even when we are consciously inclined to avoid it. Ironically, our very efforts to be humble can be tinged with a tendency to look down on other people whom we believe are not. It's what C. S. Lewis was getting at when he wrote, "A man is never so proud as when striking an attitude of humility."

> They that know God will be humble; they that know themselves cannot be proud.
>
> —John Flavel

Jesus used a story to demonstrate the irony of pride and humility in our lives—especially in our relationship with God. He told it to people who were particularly pleased with themselves:

> "Two men went up to the Temple to pray, one a Pharisee, the other a tax man. The Pharisee posed and prayed like this: 'Oh, God, I thank you that I am not like other people—robbers, crooks, adulterers, or, heaven forbid, like this tax man. I fast twice a week and tithe on all my income.'

"Meanwhile the tax man, slumped in the shadows, his face in his hands, not daring to look up, said, 'God, give mercy. Forgive me, a sinner.'"

Jesus commented, "This tax man, not the other, went home and made right with God. If you walk around with your nose in the air, you're going to end up flat on your face, but if you're content to be simply yourself, you will become more than yourself."

> A lot of men and women of doubtful reputation were hanging around Jesus.
>
> —Luke 15:1

Unhealthy pride, even for sincere God-followers, is a prevalent problem. We all struggle to strike a balance between healthy pride and healthy humility. And it becomes a surreptitious problem whenever we allow it to stand in the way of being approachable and inclusive.

How Approachable Are You?

Answer a few questions to get a bit of clarity on how inclined you currently are to open your arms and practice approachability as a means to love others. Honestly indicate how frequently you experienced each of the following over the past week. You can complete your self-test online at LoveLikeThatBook.com and receive a summary of your progress along the way.

I am known to be more inclusive than exclusive.

Never	Rarely	Sometimes	Often	Very Often

**I welcome people with differing ideas
or political viewpoints even to the point
of "turning the other cheek."**

Never	Rarely	Sometimes	Often	Very Often

I lean into humility far more than I lean into pride.

Never	Rarely	Sometimes	Often	Very Often

**I absolutely detest the idea of looking
down on others or being snobbish.**

Never	Rarely	Sometimes	Often	Very Often

**I want to include anyone who looks
to be left out or feels rejected.**

Never	Rarely	Sometimes	Often	Very Often

**I'm known by my friends as someone
who reaches out to undesirable people.**

Never	Rarely	Sometimes	Often	Very Often

**I intentionally do not size people up
by their clothes or their appearance.**

Never	Rarely	Sometimes	Often	Very Often

**I intentionally work at being less self-centered
and not feeling superior to others.**

Never	Rarely	Sometimes	Often	Very Often

**I'm the first to make sure someone in a
social setting feels accepted and included.**

Never	Rarely	Sometimes	Often	Very Often

**I work diligently to love my enemies—
the people who make my life difficult.**

Never	Rarely	Sometimes	Often	Very Often

Now take a moment to review these items. If most of your answers are "often" and "very often," you're well on your way to being approachable. Your disposition to willingly set aside your pride is strong and will serve you well. If, on the other hand, most of your answers are "never" and "rarely," you will benefit significantly from the examples and teaching that Jesus gave us on being approachable.

What Jesus Taught Us About Being Approachable

Some art scholars call it the greatest picture ever painted. It hangs in the State Hermitage Museum in Russia. Rembrandt completed the oil painting two years before his death in 1669, and he called it *The Return of the Prodigal Son*. It pulls us into the story's powerful climax—the forgiving father welcoming back his headstrong son.

Rembrandt isn't the only famous artist to depict the scene. Artists from across the ages and around the globe have been inspired by the parable Jesus told of the prodigal son. The *Expositor's Bible Commentary* calls it "the crown and flower of all the parables." As we read the account, we can't help but be captured by the story of a father's love. And, like everything Jesus taught, it carried even deeper meaning when understood in the context of first-century Palestine.

Keep in mind that Jesus told this story to Pharisees and scribes who derided Jesus for being too approachable. They murmured: "This man receives sinners and eats with them." They can't get over the fact that Jesus interacts with ungodly outcasts.

So Jesus told them a story. The parable begins with a young man, the younger of two sons, asking his father to give him his share of the family inheritance. This had to be startling to the Pharisees and scribes who were listening. Respect for one's father is paramount to the Jews. The younger son's request for his inheritance from a still-healthy patriarch constitutes an unthinkable offense. It amounts to saying, "I wish you were dead."

Still, the father agrees and gives the younger son his portion of the estate. The son quickly departs to another country where he wastes his wealth on extravagant living (the word *prodigal* actually means wasteful). After the young man's money is gone, he barely survives by taking a job feeding pigs. Hungry and penniless, he comes to his senses. He decides to go back to his father and apologize for his foolish conduct. He hopes his father will accept him, even if it's just as one of his servants.

This is where Jesus provides another surprising plot twist. The father not only accepts his son, but he's been eager to celebrate his homecoming: "When he was still a long way off, his father saw him. His heart pounding, he ran out, embraced him, and kissed him." Now, in the first century, a dignified Middle Eastern man never

"Here I am! I stand at the door and knock. If anyone hears my voice and opens the door, I will come in and eat with that person, and they with me."

—Revelation 3:20 NIV

ran. If he were to run, he would have to hitch up his tunic so he wouldn't trip. If he did this, it would show his bare legs. In that culture, it was humiliating and shameful for a man to show his bare legs. Jesus was underscoring how excited and eager the father was to see his son.

The father was most likely not only running out of excitement, however, but to catch his son before others in the village could see him. Why? Because if a Jewish son lost his inheritance among Gentiles and then returned home, the community would perform a ceremony, called the *Kezazah*. They would break a large pot in front of him to symbolize his banishment and yell, "You are now cut off from your people!" The community would totally reject him.

In Jesus' story, the father wasn't about to let that happen. So he runs to get to his son *before* he entered the village. The father runs so that his son does not experience the shame and humiliation of the community's rejection.

After this emotional reuniting of the runaway son with his father, it was clear that there would be no *Kezazah* ceremony; there would be no rejecting, only acceptance. The son had repented and returned to the father. And the father had taken the full shame that should have fallen upon his son and clearly shown to the entire community that his son was welcome back home.

The Pharisees and scribes who, moments earlier, were ridiculing Jesus for being too approachable must have been speechless. The message could not have been clearer: Jesus' love was for anyone, regardless of what laws they'd broken or sins they'd committed. Jesus was scandalously approachable because it was the very essence of his love.

How to Be More Approachable

If you want to love like that, you can't size a person up. You can't first determine if they are deserving. You can't assess whether they meet your standards before you show them love. You must be approachable—to everyone. Here's the hard truth: if you want to love like Jesus, you can't be exclusive.

Pride, as I've already noted, is the poison of love. And humility is the antidote. Humility shines a light on the dark corners of our hearts, exposing our self-centered places and extinguishing impulses of egoism and superiority. Jesus underscored this himself when he said that he came "not to be served but to serve." The apostle Paul added to this focus when he wrote, "Each of you should be concerned not only about your own interests, but the interests of others as well."

So, if we are to ever love like Jesus, we have to

> # No man is an island.
>
> —John Donne

push pride to the side and humble our hearts. That's a given. But Jesus takes it a step further. He says that if we are to be truly approachable and not exclusive we must do something outrageous. He says we must love our enemies. He says it flat out: "I tell you, love your enemies, bless those who curse you, do good to those who hate you, and pray for those who mistreat you and persecute you."

I don't know about you, but this is an incredibly tough pill to swallow. My nature is inclined to retaliate against those who mistreat me. My impulse is to even the score and then some. I understand loving your neighbor, your friends, your family, and even strangers. But enemies?

If you're thinking, like me, that Jesus may have said this flippantly, for shock value, think again. He says it more than once, and he underscores it with examples: "If someone slaps you in the face, stand there and take it. If someone grabs your shirt, giftwrap your best coat and make a present of it. If someone takes unfair advantage of you, use the occasion to practice the servant life."

The servant life? This is taking "approachability" to a radical level, isn't it? Of course. It's not natural—it's the very opposite of natural. That's why Jesus also says we can only love in this radical way when we love out of our "God-created selves." Then he tells us that God "gives his best . . . to everyone, regardless: the good and bad, the nice and nasty. If all you do is love the lovable, do you expect a bonus? Anybody can do that. If you simply say hello to those who greet you, do you expect a medal? Any run-of-the-mill sinner does that."

I get that. I'm not looking for run-of-the-mill. Like you, I'm looking for extraordinary. Like you, I aspire to love like Jesus.

So how do we do it? How do we love out of our God-created selves? I'm tempted to elaborate on the three steps Jesus recommends: *bless* those who curse you, *do good* to those who hate you, and *pray* for those who mistreat you. Bless, do good, and pray. It makes a nice sermon. And I know it proves true—especially the prayer part. "Prayer doesn't change God," said C. S. Lewis, "it changes me." But I favor the simplicity and practicality of the more succinct approach from Jesus: "Here is a simple, rule-of-thumb guide for behavior: Ask yourself what you want people to do for you, then grab the initiative and do it for *them*."

That's the key for me. More often than not, I don't even know my "enemies" until they appear right in front of me, suddenly, without warning. I need to love out of my God-created self on a moment's notice. I need

Those who
judge will never
understand,
and those who
understand will
never judge.

—Wilson Kanadi

to muster up the servant life ASAP. More often than not, I don't have the luxury of time to think through a three-step strategy. But, in my better moments, I can quickly think about what I'd want if I was the other person. And, by the way, the answer has never been a defensive or self-righteous encounter.

I've been putting this radical rule of thumb from Jesus to the test. I fail miserably, of course. Often. For example, I recently embarrassed myself by yelling out the window of my SUV at a bicyclist in slow-moving traffic who slapped my vehicle's side window because I was apparently in his space. *I'm not going to take that*, I said to myself. I hollered: "Stay in your own lane with the other bikes—that's why it's there—and don't touch my car!" So much for humility or turning the other cheek. So much for being approachable with him.

But I've also experienced some shining moments when I've tapped into my God-created self. I once received a heated email from a colleague at my university, for example, who had jumped to an irrational conclusion about the way I administered exams and assigned grades in one of my classes.

Among other things, she accused me of having our office staff grade student papers for me, a definite no-no in academic circles, and definitely something that wouldn't even enter my mind. While the accusation was erroneous, it didn't stop my colleague from launching into an in-person tirade against me. I was shocked not only by the boldness and irrationality of her accusations but by her personal attack against my character.

In fact, I was livid. *Where does this person get off making outlandish accusations about me without even checking with me first?* In that moment, she became my enemy. Everything within me was gearing up to push back. But I didn't. I made a decision to set my ego aside, as best I could, and give her what I would have wanted: warmhearted empathy.

"Molly," (not her real name) I said gently and with honest concern, "where's this anger coming from?" That was it. In that instant of genuine compassion, I was free. In that moment—the second she could see my grace-full spirit—I was giving her my best self, my God-created self. It wasn't a technique or a maneuver. I truly humbled myself, emptied myself of me in that moment. I let go of my defenses and snobbish pride. I let go of my desire to set her straight.

She apologized. "You must think I'm a lunatic," she confided. She went on to tell me how she was contending with an inordinate amount of stress. She was no longer my enemy. And I was no longer livid.

Now, I guarantee that if I had launched back at her with equally cruel comments the relationship would have been in turmoil. I would have obsessed about it, recounting what I could or should have said differently. I would have lost sleep. Mostly I would have lost out on being the kind of person I want to be. And that's something I'd be sure to regret.

In this brief passage of the Gospel According to Luke (just ten verses), where Jesus tells us to love our enemies, not just once, but twice, he closes with this:

> Give without expecting a return. You'll never—I promise—regret it. Live out this God-created identity the way our Father lives toward us, generously and graciously, even when we're at our worst. Our Father is kind; you be kind.

When we love like that, feelings of superiority fade and our days are punctuated with spontaneous breathings of compassion, generosity of spirit, and kindness. We become accessible to anyone who feels left out or unwanted. When we love like Jesus, we love without exclusion—we even love our enemies.

To Ponder

- How would you respond if you were in the experiment where everyone else voted incorrectly for the longest of three lines? Would you stick with your convictions about what you know to be true or give in to be accepted? Why or why not?

- How do you relate to Simon? If you were invited to his dinner party with Jesus, would you have understood and even sided with Simon's attempt to trap this radical person named Jesus, who was stirring up so much controversy in your temple? Or would you have been embarrassed by Simon's questions? Why?

- Jesus was incredibly inclusive of those who were rejected by most, the riffraff fringe who were rarely included by others. What about you? Do you want to have a reputation for including those who aren't typically included?

- In reading about Jesus' teaching on the prodigal son, do you identify more with the son or the father and why? In either case, what would you be thinking and feeling?

- How would you rate your current capacity to set your pride aside to be more approachable? Are you being intentional about not sizing others up by their outward appearance so you can have a welcoming spirit that makes them feel included? Why or why not?

CHAPTER 3

GRACE-FULL

Learn the unforced rhythms of grace.

—Jesus

"I'd like to see you leaning forward in your chair a bit more, Les."

I slowly scooted toward the edge of my seat, placed my elbows on my knees, and loosely touched the tips of my fingers together.

"Um. Can you not do that with your fingers? It comes off as a subtle power play."

Feeling incredibly self-conscious, I moved my hands to rest on my knees.

"Good. Now give plenty of eye contact, but don't make it a staring contest."

The coaching was coming to me through a wireless earphone from a team of three psychologists carefully observing me through a two-way mirror.

"Are you aware that you're bouncing your right foot like you're nervous?"

Well, of course I'm nervous. I'm in my first counseling session. This wasn't role-play. My patient knew he was seeing a graduate student, a psychologist-in-training, and I knew I was going to be of very little help.

I felt a little like a barber giving his first haircut—it wasn't going to be pretty.

"Remember, Les," one of my instructors whispered through my earpiece, "it's more about attitude than technique—you've got to feel a genuine sense of acceptance for this person."

They were teaching me *unconditional positive regard*, one of the fundamentals of effective counseling. The idea is to convey an authentic sense of warmth and respect for the person regardless of what they are saying or what they've done. It separates behaviors from the person in order to offer an attitude of grace.

This therapeutic approach enables a person to drop their pretenses, confess the worst parts of themselves, and discover the profound relief of knowing they are still accepted and valued as a person. It provides a judge-free space for them to reveal their faults and failings.

And if you think it's easy, think again. Why? Because

When you judge others, you do not define them, you define yourself.

—Earl Nightingale

unconditional acceptance goes against the deep grain of every human being. We're "conditional" by nature. We want people to *earn* our respect. They need to win our acceptance. We don't offer up favor without merit. And we quickly dismiss people who slip up. We like to see the penitent squirm. No matter that we have plenty of failings ourselves—judgmentalism rules our reflexes. Criticism is at the ready. Faultfinding seems bred in our bones. We like to hold people accountable, keep score. Our nature seeks fairness and justice. Not mercy and grace.

Mercy, it has been said, is getting spared from bad things you deserve. Grace is getting good things you don't deserve. As author Max Lucado puts it, "Mercy gave the Prodigal Son a second chance. Grace gave him a feast."

Grace. Of all the loving qualities that are most arresting, most striking, in the life of Christ, grace, for me, is the toughest. I love the idea of being a grace-giver. I'm with Karl Barth: "Laughter is the closest thing to the grace of God." I want more unrestrained and uproarious grace in my life. I want spontaneous moments of grace with others in my life. But I struggle, maybe like you, because grace is a gift—unconditional—and it can't be earned or achieved. It comes from a heart that requires nothing in return. Grace is, by definition, unfair. It doesn't make sense. And that's the point. If you want to love like Jesus, you can't limit your love to people who deserve it.

The Grace-Giving of Jesus

Aware of our built-in resistance to be grace-givers, Jesus modeled it time and again, perhaps nowhere more dramatically than when he's interrupted, early in the morning, while teaching in the temple. A group of puffed-up Pharisees and teachers of the law barge in on his class. They push a terrified woman in front of Jesus and his students—a woman who has been caught red-handed, guilty of adultery. Following their custom, the woman is shamed beyond humiliation by being stripped to the waist. She's defenseless, cowering before Jesus, her arms covering her bare chest.

The spectacle, from the Pharisees' perspective, is designed not so much to humiliate this woman or even punish her. They want to trap Jesus, reveal him as a heretic in front of all the people who came to hear his teaching in the temple.

Jewish law, handed down by Moses, specifies death by stoning for anyone caught in adultery. Roman law, however, forbids the Jews from carrying out executions. The Pharisees, thinking they were incredibly clever by catching Jesus off guard while he's teaching, want to

> **Anyone can find the dirt in someone. Be the one who finds the gold.**
>
> —paraphrase of Proverbs 11:27

see how he'll handle a clear-cut case of following the laws of Moses and Rome. Or, they wonder, will this rebel Jesus—notorious for merciful acts and preaching forgiveness—let the adulteress off the hook? In the mind of the Pharisees, that would settle the matter, clearly revealing Jesus as a heretic. They think they have him trapped in an impossible situation.

"Now what do you say?" they demand.

Jesus doesn't buy into their scheme. Rather than speak, Jesus bends down to write on the ground. Everyone hushes with curiosity. What's he writing? Maybe he was writing their names. Or maybe he was listing sins or other laws. The Bible doesn't say. It simply tells us that Jesus stands up and says something nobody expected: "Let any one of you who is without sin, be the first to throw a stone at her." He continues to write on the ground.

As the statement hangs in the air, these religious leaders, dressed in fine fabrics, feel as exposed as the guilty women they'd dragged into the temple. One by one, they sheepishly slip away. When it is just Jesus and the woman standing there, no more accusers to be found, Jesus asks, "Where are they? Has no one condemned you?"

"No one, sir," she answers.

"Neither do I condemn you," he tells her. "Go now and leave your life of sin."

Saved rather than stoned. The guilty woman is given grace, not guilt. And with this grace Jesus gives her new life. "Christ accepts us as we are," Walter Trobisch says, "but when he accepts us, we cannot remain as we are."

You can't study the life of Jesus and avoid life-altering grace. He is the personification of grace. He acknowledges the ugliness of sin but chooses to see beyond it. In each of the four Gospels, Jesus radiates grace not only in his teachings but in his life—toward a woman caught in adultery, a mischievous tax collector, a Roman soldier, a Samaritan woman with serial husbands, a shame-filled prostitute. Grace runs rampant in the life of Jesus. "Jesus did not identify the person with his sin," wrote theologian Helmut Thielicke, "but rather saw in this sin something alien, something that really did not belong to him, something . . . from which he would free him and bring him back to his real self."

Nowhere did Jesus more clearly separate the sin from the sinner than in the last moments of his earthly life. After unspeakable and heartless torture, Roman soldiers take Jesus the Nazarene a short distance from Jerusalem's city wall to a place the locals named Golgotha, "Place of the Skull." They initiate the barbaric ritual of nailing him to a cross. Typically, they begin by giving the victim a mild painkiller, not as an act of mercy, but to make it easier for them to nail his limbs to the wooden beams. Jesus refuses the medicine, probably to remain lucid.

Two soldiers put all their weight on his extended arms as another drives six-inch iron nails through each hand. His feet are flexed at an extreme angle, lapped one over the other, and nailed into place. They lift the cross up, guiding the base into a hole in the ground with a jarring thud. As the ruthless death squad steadies the cross to keep it upright, Jesus, who hasn't spoken in hours, whispers a prayer, "Father, forgive them, for they do not know what they are doing."

Grace beyond measure. Not only was Jesus suffering physically from this torment, he was the object of taunts and verbal abuse from the Roman killers and onlookers: "Ha! You who are going to destroy the temple and rebuild it in three days, save yourself, and come down from the cross!" The religious leaders mocked him too: "He saved others but he cannot save himself." Enduring unimaginable suffering, the Nazarene offers grace and forgiveness to his persecutors.

But his grace-giving doesn't stop there. Jesus,

He that cannot
forgive others
breaks the
bridge over
which he must
pass himself.

—Edward Herbert

thirty-three years old, hanging a few feet above the earth between two robbers, minutes before his death, has one more act of grace to give. One of the criminals hurls insults at Jesus: "Aren't you the Messiah? Save yourself and us!" The other felon rebukes his fellow crook: "We are punished justly, for we are getting what our deeds deserve. But this man has done nothing wrong."

"Jesus, remember me when you enter your kingdom," says the robber.

"Don't worry, I will. Today you will join me in paradise."

Jesus could have rained down condemnation. He could have condemned his coldhearted death squad as well as the sanctimonious leaders and this convicted criminal on a cross next to him. He could have prayed for God to strike them all down. But Jesus, the man of unconditional acceptance, even in his last breaths, gives grace.

Grace

noun
grace \'grās\

Jesus rarely used the term *grace*, but he talked about the concept frequently. Grace is most often linked with the term *favor*, as in God's "unmerited favor." It doesn't require earning merit badges. We don't have to *do something* to get it. Grace is an undeserved and unconditional gift. As Paul puts it, "For by grace you have been saved through faith, and that not of yourselves, it is the gift of God."

Trace the Greek root of *grace*, *charis*, and you will find a word meaning "cheerful or happy." Trace the same word in Hebrew, *chen*, and it means "to bend or stoop." So grace, when combining these two origins, means to happily stoop down—to gladly become inferior to another. It's ultimately what God did in sending Jesus to walk among us. "This is how God showed his love among us: He sent his one and only Son into the world that we might live through him." As Philip Yancey said in *What's So Amazing About Grace*, "While every other religion offers a way to earn approval, only Christianity dares to make God's love unconditional."

A story is told of a group of Oxford professors who were discussing the uniqueness that Christianity offered the world. Some said it was creation or the cross. Others suggested the Bible, miracles, and hope. When C. S. Lewis came in the room, the group asked him what he thought Christianity brought to

the table that other religions did not. Without hesi-
tation Lewis responded, "That's easy. It's grace."

Grace is so central to those who follow Jesus that
the apostle Paul said the church was founded on "the
gospel of the grace of God." The term *grace* occurs
well over one hundred times in the New Testament.
This gospel of grace is truly from God; humans would
have never imagined it. Our nature is to honor the
virtuous and punish the guilty. But God is happy to
give unconditional acceptance and unmerited grace
to all who will receive it.

What Keeps Us from Being Grace-Givers

If you had to rate how well you offer the benefit of the
doubt to others or how much you appreciate perspec-
tives that differ from your own, would you say you're
above average? Of course. Nobody thinks of themselves as closed-minded. That's why almost everybody
is "above average" when it comes to how they perceive
themselves.

More surprising still is that, relative to themselves,
most people think *others* suffer from judgmentalism—
but they themselves do not. Social scientists at Cornell

University discovered this fact when testing people's competency levels. They concluded their study by saying, "Incompetent people don't know they're incompetent."

I suppose it makes sense. We'd rather believe good things about ourselves than face the truth that we are pietistic or judgmental. So we deceive ourselves. And self-deception is a stepping stone to self-righteousness. It rubs us the wrong way to admit our faults—even to ourselves. Not because we are narcissists. It's because we are human. We dismiss whatever doesn't jive with our self-image by seeing bad qualities in others. We do it without a second thought. In fact, we do it without a conscious thought:

- **Why can't that mother control her unruly kids?** Unconsciously we're saying: "I wish I was a better mom, and when I judge this woman who appears to be struggling, I feel better about myself."
- **That guy is constantly smiling—it's so obnoxious and phony.** Unconsciously: "I wish I was a happier person. But since I'm not, I may feel better by judging him to be a fraud."
- **What a bunch of angry losers out there protesting on the streets—they need to get a job.** Unconsciously: "Their conviction and activism scares me, but by calling them lazy I feel morally superior."

Social scientists call it *negativity bias*. The rest of us call it judgmentalism. Like me, I'm guessing you don't think of yourself as judgmental. It's other people who are that way, right? But let's be honest. Judgmental thoughts shoot through everyone's mind. Lurking just beneath the surface of our conscious thinking, we think: *I'm shocked and aghast by that person's behavior; I wouldn't think of doing such a thing.* We need to clearly note how different we are from others who do despicable things. We want to underscore to ourselves that we would never sink to their level. It's a defensive move to protect our own "purity," says author Terry Cooper. "We *need* other people's faults in order to dodge our own." Judgmentalism finds its identity in what it *is not*.

> O momentary grace of mortal men / Which we more hunt for than the grace of God.
>
> —William Shakespeare

For this reason, we call on judgmentalism whenever we feel insecure. It puffs us up, feeding our self-deception, telling us we are superior. Like a drug that instantly relieves our pain, we tear others down to build ourselves up. We know the wise teaching: "Do not judge, or you too will be judged." But we are addicted to our delusion.

Judgmentalism has a hold on us. We are mistaken to

believe otherwise. We may think we are above average when it comes to being nonjudgmental, but as Byron Langenfeld says, "Rare is the person who can weigh the faults of others without putting his thumb on the scales."

Judgmentalism will always be part of us. We will always suffer from moral spasms of self-righteous judgment. The answer? Being *less* judgmental. Taking our thumb off the scales of judgmentalism is the goal. Why? Because judgmentalism keeps us from becoming better grace-givers. You can't give grace while feeling self-righteous. Grace comes only from a humble heart.

How Grace-Full Are You?

Take a moment to honestly indicate how frequently you experienced each of the following over the past week, and it will give you a little clarity on how inclined you currently are to open your heart to others. You can complete your self-test online at LoveLikeThatBook.com and receive a summary of your progress along the way.

I don't focus on having other people earn my respect—I just give it to them.

Never	Rarely	Sometimes	Often	Very Often

**I stay completely clear of
criticizing others and faultfinding.**

| Never | Rarely | Sometimes | Often | Very Often |

Like Jesus, I separate the sin from the sinner.

| Never | Rarely | Sometimes | Often | Very Often |

**I give love, respect, and appreciation
freely to people who don't deserve it.**

| Never | Rarely | Sometimes | Often | Very Often |

**People who know me well would
describe me as a grace-giver.**

| Never | Rarely | Sometimes | Often | Very Often |

I know God loves me unconditionally.

| Never | Rarely | Sometimes | Often | Very Often |

**When I see someone acting in a way I don't
like, I'm inclined to give them the benefit of the
doubt until I better understand the situation.**

| Never | Rarely | Sometimes | Often | Very Often |

**I feel God's love in my life and know I
receive it even when I don't deserve it.**

Never	Rarely	Sometimes	Often	Very Often

**I'm more inclined to have an open
heart than an accusing finger.**

Never	Rarely	Sometimes	Often	Very Often

**I believe the best about people. Even if
they've been bad, I want the best for them.**

Never	Rarely	Sometimes	Often	Very Often

If most of your answers are "often" and "very often," you're well on your way to having an open heart full of grace. Your disposition to willingly set aside judgmentalism and give people the benefit of the doubt is strong and will serve you well. If, on the other hand, most of your answers are "never" and "rarely," you will benefit significantly from Jesus' teaching on being more accepting and grace-full.

What Jesus Taught Us About Giving Grace

On a trip to Rome, I received special permission to tour the Vatican Scavi, two floors beneath the massive

St. Peter's Basilica in Vatican City. Believed to be the resting place of Jesus' first disciple, Peter, the partially excavated mausoleum is found by walking along a narrow and dimly lit underground street in the ancient city of the dead. The streets of the necropolis are similar to those of ancient Rome, only they are flanked by tombs instead of shops and apartments. Greek graffiti on the wall marks the spot: "Peter is within."

Something about walking along that street and standing in that place, the very spot where Peter was martyred two thousand years ago, caused me to think about Peter's relationship with Jesus the Nazarene. Peter, more than any other disciple, experienced grace on a personal level from Jesus. After all, Peter denied knowing Jesus even after declaring, "I will never disown you." The emotional turmoil behind Peter's denial and later repentance and acceptance from Jesus are all the more meaningful when you consider a question he blurted out to Jesus one day: "We left everything and followed you. What do we get out of it?"

Peter is a man after my own heart. I would have been asking the same question.

Jesus understood Peter's question and, in his trademark teaching style, Jesus told Peter a story of an estate manager who hired workers for his vineyards early in the morning. They agreed on a dollar a day and went to work.

To love a person means to see him as God intended him to be.

—Fyodor Dostoevsky

Later, about nine that morning, the manager saw some other men hanging around the town square, unemployed. So he hired them. He did the same thing at noon and again at three o'clock. And at five. They all went to work in his vineyard. When the day's work was over, the owner of the vineyard instructed his foreman, "Call the workers in and pay them their wages. Start with the last hired and go on to the first."

"Those hired at five o'clock came up and were each given a dollar. When those who were hired first saw that, they assumed they would get far more. But they got the same, each of them one dollar. Taking the dollar, they groused angrily to the manager, 'These last workers put in only one easy hour, and you just made them equal to us, who slaved all day under a scorching sun.'

"He replied to the one speaking for the rest, 'Friend, I haven't been unfair. We agreed on the wage of a dollar, didn't we? So take it and go. I decided to give to the one who came last the same as you. Can't I do what I want with my own money? Are you going to get stingy because I am generous?'"

Talk about unconventional. If Peter was looking for a benefit plan in this parable, he didn't find the one he was expecting. Thinking he'd worked longer and harder than others, Peter assumed, like all of us, that he'd be rewarded accordingly. But the Grace-Giver from Nazareth doesn't work according to a tiered system of reward. That's not how his vineyard operates.

If you think you deserve more than others, you've forgotten how you got into the vineyard in the first place. When you compare your performance with others, you miss the point of the pay plan. Grace is not dependent on the hours you work, the results you produce, or the job you do. That's why in this grace-filled vineyard the first are last and the last are first. It defies logic.

In another parable, Jesus warned that farmers who concentrate on pulling up weeds may destroy the wheat along with the weeds. His point? Judgmentalism uproots grace. Leave matters of judgment to the one true Judge.

Jesus talked often about grace—though he almost never used the word. He spoke in stories that illustrated it. But in some situations, he didn't mince words about criticizing others. He delivered a clear message about judgmentalism in his Sermon on the Mount:

> "Don't pick on people, jump on their failures, criticize their faults—unless, of course, you want the same treatment. That critical spirit has a way of boomeranging. It's easy to see a smudge on your neighbor's face and be oblivious to the ugly sneer on your own. Do you have the nerve to say, 'Let me wash your face for you,' when your own face

is distorted by contempt? It's this whole traveling road-show mentality all over again, playing a holier-than-thou part instead of just living your part. Wipe that ugly sneer off your own face, and you might be fit to offer a washcloth to your neighbor."

No need for interpretation here. Hypocrisy and self-righteousness are nonstarters for Jesus. Quit nitpicking. Quit tearing down others to boost yourself up. You can't be hypercritical *and* a grace-giver. It's an impossibility. If you judge others with a holier-than-thou attitude, you are sure to be judged in the same way. Jesus doesn't mince his words when it comes to judgmentalism negating grace.

How to Be a Better Grace-Giver

I had just stepped onto the platform in the Rose Garden Arena in Portland, Oregon, where nearly ten thousand people had assembled for a marriage seminar. That night each of the six speakers was to give a brief overview of what we would be speaking on over the next couple of days. Just before the rest of us went to the podium, my friend Gary Smalley captivated the crowd by holding up a crisp fifty-dollar bill and asking the massive audience, "Who would like this fifty-dollar bill?" Hands started going up everywhere. He said, "I am going to give this fifty dollars to one of you, but first let me do this." He proceeded to crumple up the bill. Then he asked, "Who still wants it?" The same hands went up in the air.

"Well," he replied, "what if I do this?" He dropped it on the ground and started to grind it into the floor with his shoe. He picked it up, all crumpled and dirty. "Now who still wants it?" Again, hands went into the air. "You have all learned a valuable lesson," Gary said. "No matter what I do to the money, you still want it because it doesn't decrease in value. It is still worth fifty dollars."

> "Forgive them. They don't know what they're doing."
>
> —Jesus

Gary's simple illustration underscores a profound point. Many times in our lives we are dropped, crumpled, and ground into the dirt by the decisions we make or the circumstances that come our way. We may feel as though we are worthless, insignificant in our own and in others' eyes. But no matter what has happened or what will happen, we never lose our value if we choose to receive God's grace.

Perhaps you've already internalized the message that crowd in Portland heard, and you already have a profound sense of God's grace in your life. Maybe you already know at the center of your being, deep down in your soul, that your value is established for all time. Your *lovability* is rooted deep in God's unending love for you. You don't have to work harder, look better, or win prizes of any kind. You know and live the most crucial message ever articulated: that you have inestimable worth because you are a creation of the Creator.

Chances are, however, that even if you have experienced this grace at *some* time, you don't feel unconditionally loved by God *all* the time. Research reveals that while many of us have heard the truth about our worth in God's eyes, most of us, most of the time, aren't able to incorporate it into our everyday lives. It doesn't seem to really make a difference. We hear the message. We agree with it. And that's that. But instead of being unswervingly confident of our unconditional acceptance—feeling it resonate deep within our bones every day—we fall back into the habit of trying to earn it. Even if we agree that our Creator loves us, we still end up feeling better about ourselves only when we are winning the approval of others.

We seem to be on a cosmic quest to *establish* our value—to prove it, earn it, deserve it. And once we find what we're looking for, we relax—but only momentarily. Eventually the people we are pleasing—whether a parent, a spouse, a friend, an advisory board, or an

I do not at all
understand the
mystery of grace—
only that it meets
us where we are but
does not leave us
where it found us.

—Anne Lamott

audience—quit sending us *love messages*. Ultimately we find ourselves back on our endless quest. And that unfulfilling quest makes it nearly impossible to love like Jesus. Why? Because we can't give grace to others when we aren't receiving it ourselves. When we're busy earning acceptance from God, we start to think everyone else should earn it too. Judgmentalism creeps in. Self-righteousness appears.

If you want to be a better grace-giver, you've got to continually and consciously receive the grace God gives you. "Whoever has been forgiven only a little," Jesus said, "loves only a little." The more grace we receive, the more love we give. When we aren't cognizant of God's unconditional acceptance in our own lives, we can't give it to others. Judgmentalism sees to that.

Here's the truth: God's grace is received, not achieved. Grace does not depend on what we have done for God but rather what God has done for us. And continually receiving God's grace—in the deepest and most central parts of our beings—is the only true and lasting remedy to ugly judgments and holier-than-thou attitudes. "To be a Christian means to forgive the inexcusable," said C. S. Lewis, "because God has forgiven the inexcusable in you."

Love is not the cause of grace. It's the proof of it. When we are conscious of God's grace in our own lives, we are automatically more loving and accepting of others. I'm not naive about our judgments. I don't think it's possible to live a life where we never judge anyone, ever. But once you embrace God's grace, once you raise your consciousness around this gift you are continually given, you get immeasurably closer to loving like Jesus.

Grace, ultimately, is a choice. Clara Barton, founder of the Red Cross, was talking with a friend one day when the name of a person they both knew came up. Years before that person had treated Clara in a terribly unkind way. The friend asked Barton, "Don't you remember when she did that to you?"

> **All human nature vigorously resists grace because grace changes us and the change is painful.**
>
> —Flannery O'Connor

"No," Barton replied, "I distinctly remember forgetting that."

Clara Barton made a choice. A tough choice. And it's the same one you and I make whenever we offer grace. I've learned a way to make this tough choice a little easier, however. It has to do with curiosity. "Curiosity," said Albert Einstein, "has its own reason for existing." And maybe this is it. The next time you sense a judgmental spasm in your heart, conjure curiosity. Why? Because curiosity squelches criticism and stiff-arms judgmentalism. Curiosity creates a space for grace. How? Almost every evaluation we make of others arises from incomplete information. We fill in the gaps of what we don't know with prejudicial judgments. Curiosity, however, keeps our judgments at bay. It opens our mind to the possibility that there is something about the situation we don't fully understand.

When you see someone you *think* is acting insane, stupid, or worse—this is the question: "I wonder what's going on with that person that I don't know about?" This little question is an accelerant to grace and a deterrent to sanctimony.

But don't be fooled. Asking yourself this curiosity question isn't easy. Judging people is easy. The question requires work. It demands empathy and a healthy dose of self-control. You have to press your emotional pause button. You have to wait a beat. Someone makes a vicious comment about another person who doesn't deserve it—maybe it's you. You want to lash out. But you pause. "Why would a grown person act in such a mean-spirited way?" That's it. This curious question is all it takes to put a haughty spirit of self-righteous judgment on hold. This question ushers guilt to the side and gives grace the opportunity to enter the scene.

A rabbi taught that experiences of God can never be

To err
is human;
to forgive,
infrequent.

—Franklin P. Adams

planned or achieved. "They are spontaneous moments of grace, almost accidental."

His student asked, "Rabbi, if God-realization is just accidental, why do we work so hard doing all these spiritual practices?"

The rabbi replied, "To be as accident-prone as possible."

The same is true of spontaneous moments of grace—those moments where we replace condemnation with undeserved love. You see, the more we practice curiosity, the more likely grace is to infuse our relationships. And the more likely we are to love like Jesus.

To Ponder

- What do you make of the sentiment that says mercy is getting spared from bad things you deserve, and grace is getting good things you don't deserve? Do you agree? Why or why not?
- Put yourself in the temple classroom where Jesus was teaching when the religious leaders brought in a woman caught in adultery. Can you imagine? What would be going through your mind as they put Jesus on the spot? Would you have agreed with the grace-giving response of Jesus to this woman?

- Do you think you are above average when it comes to being nonjudgmental? Most people think they are more grace-giving than they actually are. Why is that? And what can you do, in practical terms, to keep your own judgmentalism in view?

- In this grace-filled vineyard that Jesus described in a parable to Peter and the other disciples, he said the first are last and the last are first. How does that sit with you? Be honest. Does it rub you the wrong way? What is the main lesson from this parable for you personally?

- Chances are that you believe God loves you. Right? But when it comes down to it, are you like most others who continue to really think you have to earn God's love? In what ways do you fall for this biblical misnomer? And do you believe that receiving God's unconditional love on a personal level becomes the fuel for loving others unconditionally?

CHAPTER 4

BOLD

Your task is to be true, not popular.

—Jesus

You're sitting in a large lecture hall listening to an incredibly complicated lecture. After thirty minutes of incomprehensible jibber-jabber, the lecturer pauses and asks if there are any questions. No hands go up.

You look around the room. Could these people really understand what the lecturer is talking about? You yourself are completely lost. Your fear of looking stupid keeps you from raising your hand, but as you look around the room at your passive classmates, you assume they understand the lecture. Otherwise they'd ask questions. But they're feeling the same way you do.

They're not asking questions because nobody's asking questions.

Social scientists call it *pluralistic ignorance*. And it occurs whenever a group of people go along with something because they incorrectly assume everyone else understands or accepts it. Pluralistic ignorance leads corporations to persist in failing strategies and governments to persist in unpopular foreign policies. It leads good-intentioned worshippers to go along with unhealthy religious leadership. Pluralistic ignorance persists. It persists until someone is bold enough to speak out.

Hans Christian Andersen, the Danish writer famous for his fairy tales, memorialized the phenomenon in 1835—long before scientists labeled it—in his fable "The Emperor's New Clothes." You've heard the story before, but probably as a child.

A narcissistic emperor surrounds himself with people who only say what he wants to hear. Even the browbeaten citizens of the empire are so cowering and timid that they dare not disagree with the emperor's edicts, nor will they criticize anything he says or does.

Then two con men appear on the scene. They witness the ridiculous situation in the empire and realize they can make a fast buck. They announce that they are the world's best tailors and offer to make wonderful garments for the emperor—clothing such as has never been seen before. The catch is that the price tag for

There is nothing more frightening than active ignorance.

—Johann Wolfgang von Goethe

such royal garments is exorbitant. And as vanity will have it, the emperor insists that they make him new clothes.

After collecting a huge fee, the con men go to work, miming the actions of tailors. The emperor is measured and fitted, refitted and remeasured. The kingdom awaits breathlessly the day when the emperor will appear in his new duds, for word has it that only men of the purest of hearts will be able to see the glorious clothing in which the emperor will make his debut.

Finally, the day comes, and the emperor is dressed in his new clothes. Everyone compliments the emperor on his stunning appearance as he strolls regally through his capital city.

Unbeknownst to his people, however, the emperor is having some doubts about his own purity of heart. He can't see his new clothes. Knowing that he cannot allow his people to see his own consternation, he goes along with the ploy. The crowd becomes more and more enthralled with his new outfit. Then suddenly, from somewhere back in the crowd, a young boy shouts, "The emperor has no clothes!"

The emperor is horrified. The crowd is dismayed. But slowly it begins to dawn on everyone present: Who has a purer heart than a child? Sure enough, the emperor has no clothes. Everyone was thinking it. But nobody was bold enough to say it. They were going along with the absurdity purely because they didn't have the gumption to speak the truth.

And so was born a lesson for the ages—you can't shy away from what is true; it requires boldness. But long before this legend was ever written, Jesus confronted a similar lack of congruence in his own religious culture. In fact, he boldly shattered the pluralistic ignorance of his time. He was fearless when it came to being real, authentic, and truthful.

If you want to love like Jesus, you can't shy away from what you know is right and true. You can't remain silent just to go unnoticed. Loving like Jesus is not for the chickenhearted. It requires a fierce commitment to being authentic. It requires a bold commitment to being a truth-teller.

The Bold Truth-Telling of Jesus

As I study the life of Jesus—how he loved others in practical ways—the most startling quality I find is authenticity. While often serene and peaceful, he didn't shy away from showdowns. He corrected his disciples. He spoke his mind. No one accused him of being a pushover—or winsome. He was a straight shooter. He didn't dance around what needed to be said—he said it. He made others feel uncomfortable, if necessary. He never allowed truth to take a back seat to politeness. He never backed down from confrontation.

The group Jesus confronted most was the group that he most resembled. Of all the religious groups of his time—including the Sadducees, Samaritans, Herodians, Essenes, and Zealots—scholars agree that Jesus, the rabbi from Nazareth, most closely matched the profile of a Pharisee. He obeyed the Mosaic law, quoted leading Pharisees, and often took their side in public arguments. The Pharisees devoted their lives to following God, tithed to the penny, and obeyed the strict laws of the Torah. They held to traditional values and were model citizens.

> **To ignore evil is to become an accomplice to it.**
>
> —Martin Luther King Jr.

Yet Jesus singled out the Pharisees more than any other group for his strongest critiques and confrontations. No one dared challenge the Pharisees until Jesus. And he didn't hold back. He boldly called them hypocrites and even a brood of vipers. He said to them: "You strain out a gnat but swallow a camel." Or as another translation puts it:

"You religion scholars and Pharisees! Frauds! You keep meticulous account books, tithing on every

nickel and dime you get, but on the meat of God's
Law, things like fairness and compassion and
commitment—the absolute basics!—you carelessly
take it or leave it. Careful bookkeeping is com-
mendable, but the basics are required."

Jesus condemned their legalism, mostly, and their
emphasis on externals: "You Pharisees clean the outside
of the cup and dish, but inside you are full of greed and
wickedness." He pointed out that they were focused
more on impressing others than loving God. He clearly
denounced this kind of external showmanship in his
Sermon on the Mount:

"When you do something for someone else, don't
call attention to yourself. You've seen them in
action, I'm sure—'playactors' I call them—treating
prayer meeting and street corner alike as a stage,
acting compassionate as long as someone is watching, playing to the crowds. They get applause, true,
but that's all they get. When you help someone out,
don't think about how it looks. Just do it—quietly
and unobtrusively. That is the way your God, who
conceived you in love, working behind the scenes,
helps you out.

"And when you come before God, don't turn
that into a theatrical production either. All these

people making a regular show out of their prayers, hoping for stardom! Do you think God sits in a box seat?

"Here's what I want you to do: Find a quiet, secluded place so you won't be tempted to role-play before God. Just be there as simply and honestly as you can manage. The focus will shift from you to God, and you will begin to sense his grace."

For Jesus, the proof of spiritual maturity is not external. Spirituality is not for show. It's an inside job. He abhorred hypocrisy and never backed away from confronting it. He took on hecklers and scoffers of every stripe. But nowhere was he more aggressive, nowhere more shockingly confrontational than when he clenched a whip in his fist and made his way up the temple steps during a Passover celebration.

As many as four million Jewish believers, traveling from Galilee, Syria, Egypt, and even Rome, celebrate this climax of the Jewish year in Jerusalem. Not that they have a choice. Not visiting the temple during Passover is one of thirty-six transgressions that results in being spiritually cut off from God. So, as he has done every spring since childhood, Jesus made his way to Jerusalem to visit the temple. But this Passover will not be like any other.

Jewish law forbade idolatrous images—even on

To see injustice and do nothing about that means to participate in it.

—Jean-Jacques Rousseau

coins. So out-of-towners waited in line to exchange their meager savings of Roman coins for shekels, the standard currency of Jerusalem. It's the only coin accepted for paying the annual tax or for purchasing animals for ritual sacrifice. The scheming money changers charged exorbitant rates for this exchange, driving many worshippers into debt, causing them to lose their homes, land, and livestock. The money changers, in cahoots with the temple high priests who share the profits, know it's a religious scam.

The temple priests and their Roman masters make even more money when the poor buy a mandatory animal sacrifice, a lamb or a dove, only to have a priest inspect it to find a blemish, deeming it unclean and requiring the peasant to buy another.

Jesus couldn't take it. The corruption made his blood boil. He hadn't preached a single message before a crowd at this point. He had not challenged Rome or the temple's high priests. Most would have no idea who he is. And nothing in his behavior so far has been rebellious or even confrontational. But now, as he walks past the helpless people standing before the greedy money changers and sanctimonious high priests overseeing them, the normally peaceful Nazarene snaps. Steely eyed, he storms the money changers' tables, places two hands underneath the nearest one, and flips it. A small fortune of coins scatters in every direction. As people gasp in shock, Jesus is on to the next table. And the next. He cracks his whip, sending the sacrificial goats and sheep running.

Nobody stops him. "How dare you turn my Father's house into a market," he screams.

Men who enjoyed power over the pilgrims just moments earlier now cower, terrified that Jesus will turn the whip on them. The temple courts are so vast that Jesus' outburst goes unheard by the priests and worshippers within the temple itself. But the poor and oppressed who have witnessed Jesus' act of defiance know they have seen something extraordinary. Many of them have long dreamed of committing such a bold act. They are astonished. From his Galilean accent and simple robes, they know he is one of them.

Of course, this is the rarest of experiences for Jesus. There's nothing else like it in any of the Gospels. But there are numerous confrontational encounters. Not only did he correct false teachings on numerous occasions, he boldly silenced the chief priests, scribes, Pharisees,

> **Those who make peaceful revolution impossible will make violent revolution inevitable.**
>
> —John F. Kennedy

and Sadducees by putting them in their place with Scripture. He exposed their true motives. A self-seeking man boastfully promised to follow Jesus anywhere because he thought it would mean political or financial gain for him. Jesus corrected his wrong motives by telling him that he would be following a homeless Messiah. Jesus corrected Martha's anxious heart by pointing to her sister sitting at his feet and listening to him. He basically said, "You should be more like your sister." And while he had more tenderness and patience with his disciples, he sometimes rebuked and confronted their actions too.

In short, Jesus is the ultimate truth-teller. Courageous. Confident. Bold. He is a model for living authentically and honestly.

Bold

adjective
bold \'bōld\

In the pilot episode of his political satire program *The Colbert Report*, comedian Stephen Colbert coined a playful word that stuck: *truthiness*. In fact, the term was named Word of the Year for 2006 by *Merriam-Webster*. It has to do with a "truth" that a person claims to know intuitively because it "feels right." It was Colbert's jab at those who make impassioned arguments based on "facts" that don't exist. It's the exact opposite of trustworthy.

Look up the term *truthful*, on the other hand, and you'll find a variety of synonyms: *bona fide*, *genuine*, *real*, *sincere*, *true*, and *unquestionable*. But you'll also find a phrase that appears under this word in nearly every dictionary: "worthy of trust." The phrase cuts to the heart of what it means to be a bold truth-teller. In fact, the Germanic origins convey the notion being "steadfast as an oak." Solid. Reliable. Strong.

The word *authentic* derives from the Greek work *anyein* and means "to accomplish." And anyone who has become worthy of trust in the eyes of others has accomplished a great deal. When you are genuine, when you are true to your convictions, it shows. You speak up. You make a difference. People respect you—even if they disagree. They know you live not by what "feels right" but by what *is* right.

What Keeps Us from Being Bold Truth-Tellers?

"You're the first person I have ever been completely honest with." Every psychologist hears these words

We often err not because we find it hard to perceive the truth (it is often right there, at the surface), but because it is easier and more pleasant to be guided by our feelings, especially if self-centered.

—Alexander Solzhenitsyn

from time to time, but it was Sidney Jourard who made sense of them in his in-depth book *The Transparent Self*. He was puzzled over the frequency with which patients were more honest and authentic with a clinician than they were with family or friends. After much study, he concluded that each of us has a natural, built-in desire to be known, but we often stifle our vulnerability out of fear.

Fear of what? In a word, rejection. We're afraid of being seen as too emotional or not emotional enough, as too assertive or not assertive enough, too whatever or not whatever enough. We're afraid of being alienated, losing approval and acceptance. The result? We wear masks. We become what Abraham Maslow called "jellyfish in armor" by pretending to be fine when we're not, by acting indifferent when something truly irks us, and by clamming up when we really have something to say. Ultimately, we wear masks when we accept pluralistic ignorance.

We vacillate between the impulse to reveal ourselves and the impulse to protect ourselves. We seesaw between remaining mum and speaking the truth. In a seemingly inexplicable paradox, we long both to be known and to remain hidden. If we wear our masks long enough, we may guard against rejection, but we'll never be true. We'll never be honest. We'll never be bold. And that means we'll never love like Jesus.

In fact, Jesus put his finger squarely on the reason we shy away from truth-telling:

"There's trouble ahead when you live only for the approval of others, saying what flatters them, doing what indulges them. Popularity contests are not truth contests—look how many scoundrel preachers were approved by your ancestors! Your task is to be true, not popular."

Here's the situation: when what you do and what you say do not match the person you are inside—when your truth is not revealed to others—you develop an incongruent or fragmented self. Your outside doesn't match what's going on inside. You're consumed with the impression you're making on others rather than being true to who you are. You're asking *How am I doing?* instead of *How is this person doing?*

In *Traveling Mercies*, Anne Lamott writes, "Everything is usually so masked or perfumed or disguised in the world, and it's so touching when you get to see something real and human . . . no

> **One must not conceal any part of what one has recognized to be true.**
>
> —Albert Einstein

matter how neurotic the member [of the group], how deeply annoying or dull . . . when people have seen you at your worst, you don't have to put on the mask as much. And that gives us license to try on that radical hat of liberation, that hat of self-acceptance."

Being congruent—allowing your real self to match the self you're presenting to others—liberates prideful pretensions and boldly reveals the true you.

How Bold Are You?

If you're curious to get a little snapshot of how inclined you currently are to practice mindfulness in order to love others well, take a moment to honestly indicate how frequently you experienced each of the following over the past week. You can complete your self-test online at LoveLikeThatBook. com and receive a summary of your progress along the way.

**My friends would say I'm transparent,
straightforward, and direct.**

Never	Rarely	Sometimes	Often	Very Often

If I have a problem with someone, I meet with
them as soon as I can to get it ironed out
(rather than sulking or whining about it).

Never   Rarely   Sometimes   Often   Very Often

I speak out if someone is not being treated
fairly—even if it means risking rejection.

Never   Rarely   Sometimes   Often   Very Often

I'm bold when it comes to saying what needs
to be said or doing what needs to be done.

Never   Rarely   Sometimes   Often   Very Often

When my conviction is strong, I couldn't
care less what others think of me.

Never   Rarely   Sometimes   Often   Very Often

I feel urgent about making things right when
something is wrong in one of my relationships—I
take immediate action to make it better.

Never   Rarely   Sometimes   Often   Very Often

I feel congruent between my real
self and the self I present to others.

Never   Rarely   Sometimes   Often   Very Often

I sometimes make people feel uncomfortable because I'm a straight shooter who doesn't put up with deceit or hypocrisy.

Never	Rarely	Sometimes	Often	Very Often

I'd rather be genuine than win approval.

Never	Rarely	Sometimes	Often	Very Often

I'm not afraid of rejection by others.

Never	Rarely	Sometimes	Often	Very Often

Now take a moment to review these items. If most of your answers are "often" and "very often," you're well on your way to being bold—you're willing to risk rejection to bring about relational truth. If, on the other hand, most of your answers are "never" and "rarely," you will benefit significantly from Jesus' teaching on being bold.

What Jesus Taught Us About Boldly Speaking the Truth

ABC News correspondent John Quiñones began hosting a hidden-camera television program in 2008 called *What Would You Do?* The show became a hit as it featured actors acting out troubling scenes in public places while hidden cameras captured the responses of unknowing real-life bystanders. Each episode concludes with the host poignantly asking viewers: "What would you do?" It's a question that helps us contend with our personal reactions to injustice and wrong-doing. Would we likely give into bystander apathy or would we speak out and intervene? In a sense, studying the life of Jesus, the predicaments and situations that emerge in his journey, evokes the same question—especially when his truth-telling causes embarrassment and discomfort. As I read the Gospels, I ask myself the question time and again: *What would I do?*

I cringe at my own sheepish inclinations to take the easy way out in these situations where Jesus is so transparent. At the same time, I recoil at the idea of being as forthright as he is. Consider how he handles the insulting treatment from his dinner host, Simon. When Jesus realizes Simon invited him to his house to embarrass him and reveal him as a heretic, Jesus calls him out right there and then. Would you do that? I'd complain to friends about it later on, for sure. But confront my host directly in the moment? That's what Jesus did. Simon's immoral behavior is being masqueraded as goodness, and Jesus wants no part of the charade. To remain silent would be the same as

It is better to

be divided by

truth than to be

united in error.

—Adrian Rodgers

endorsing his conniving behavior. So he confronts it—just as he does with Zacchaeus, Martha, the woman at the well, the chief priests, and on and on. Even his own disciples.

Before you chalk up this forthright approach to being a personality issue more than a mandate, consider the straightforward teaching of Jesus on the matter: "If a fellow believer hurts you, go and tell him—work it out between the two of you." There's an urgency to this truth-telling. And Jesus even prioritizes it over our worship: "If you enter your place of worship and, about to make an offering, you suddenly remember a grudge a friend has against you, abandon your offering, leave immediately, go to this friend and make things right. Then and only then, come back and work things out with God."

It's clear that, for Jesus, truth-telling is not something we do when we get around to it. He makes it a top priority: "Don't lose a minute," he says. "Make the first move; make things right." Jesus doesn't tell us to ruminate on it. Gossip about it. No. He says we need to speak the truth but with love: "Confront him with the need for repentance, and offer again God's forgiving love."

Truth without love is ugly, and love without truth is spineless. As the ancient proverb says: "Faithful are the wounds of a friend [who corrects out of love and concern], but the kisses of an enemy are deceitful [because they serve his hidden agenda]."

Jesus is all about authenticity. He wants us to take off our masks and live congruent lives without hidden agendas or empty promises:

> **Peace if possible, truth at all costs.**
>
> —Martin Luther

"Don't say anything you don't mean. This counsel is embedded deep in our traditions. You only make things worse when you lay down a smoke screen of pious talk, saying, 'I'll pray for you,' and never doing it, or saying, 'God be with you,' and not meaning it. You don't make your words true by embellishing them with religious lace. In making your speech sound more religious, it becomes less true. Just say 'yes' and 'no.' When you manipulate words to get your own way, you go wrong."

Early in his ministry, while in Galilee, Jesus meets a man named Nathanael. His brother, Philip, has invited Nathanael to "come and see" the man he and his friends have met, a man who has already stirred their faith and hope. Nathanael scoffs but goes with them. As Nathanael approaches, Jesus says of him, "Here is truly an Israelite in whom there is no deceit!"

Jesus is engaging in some clever wordplay—these men would have known that their ancestor Israel, formerly Jacob, was known as the "deceiver" because of the ways he tricked his brother, Esau, and his father, Isaac. But Jesus is also commenting on the observed character of Nathanael, declaring him to be a man in whom there is nothing false. Nathanael is honest and direct; he says what he thinks ("Can anything good come out of Nazareth?"). He responds with openness to his brother's invitation to explore a fresh opportunity for growth by meeting this new rabbi. And Jesus praises Nathanael for this.

Jesus himself lived in a way that was utterly transparent, straightforward, and direct, and he wants us to follow in this way. Not only does a life marked by truth-telling open us up to the richness of our spiritual relationship with God, but it also empowers us to live meaningfully and lovingly with each other.

How to Be a Better and Bolder Truth-Teller

"Real isn't how you are made. It's a thing that happens to you," said the toy horse. "When a child loves you for a long, long time, not just to play with, but really loves you, then you become Real."

This old toy horse in Margery Williams's classic

children's book *The Velveteen Rabbit* squarely identifies the fact that we are most real when we are most known and loved. It's synergistic. The more real we become, the more love we experience. And the more love we experience, the more real we become.

The toy rabbit didn't know real rabbits existed. He thought they were all stuffed with sawdust like himself. "And he understood that sawdust was quite out-of-date and should never be mentioned in modern circles." The rabbit kept authenticity at bay through his fear of being found out. He never wanted to risk being *really* known. And yet authenticity is the only way to be loved.

That's the irony. We fear that being known will lead to rejection. It will get our vulnerable hearts kicked across the floor. But it is only by being known that our hearts are truly loved.

C. S. Lewis, as he so often does, puts his finger on a truth that resonates:

> To love at all is to be vulnerable. Love anything, and your heart will be wrung and possibly be broken. If you want to be sure of keeping [your heart] intact, you must give your heart to no one, not even to an animal. Wrap it carefully around with hobbies and little luxuries; avoid all entanglements; lock it up safely in the casket or coffin of your selfishness. But in that casket—safe, dark, motionless, airless—it

A "no" uttered from deepest conviction is better and greater than a "yes" merely uttered to please, or what is worse, to avoid trouble.

—Mahatma Gandhi

will change. It will not be broken; it will become unbreakable, impenetrable, irredeemable. . . . The only place outside of Heaven where you can be perfectly safe from the dangers . . . of love is Hell.

Each time we pass up an urge to be a truth-teller, we face a greater danger than being rejected. We risk a hardened heart that prevents the risk of love. We fall victim to the proverbial disease to please. Authenticity separates *being* a loving person from merely wanting to *seen* as a loving person. When you are real, your head and heart work in harmony. You are the same person behind the curtain as you are on stage. You no longer perform to win love. Instead, you risk rejection to be loving.

Authenticity is all about *being* rather than *doing*. When you give attention to truth-telling from a loving heart, your actions naturally follow. They are not contrived. There's no pretense. No show. You don't wonder what you should do. Your *doing* flows naturally from your *being*.

Here's the hard truth: love is dangerous because love means risking rejection. Jesus fearlessly risked not only his reputation but his very life for the truth.

> ## It matters enormously if I alienate anyone from the truth.
>
> —C. S. Lewis

This uncompromising quality can leave some people uncomfortable. No doubt. But that discomfort just may be the most loving thing we can do for them. The Pharisees, the group Jesus most often criticized, actually praised Jesus for not being swayed by people's opinions. It's the only compliment they ever gave him.

So, if you want to become a better and bolder truth-teller, a good place to start is with a little more vulnerability. Why? Because, like Margery Williams's rabbit, we keep authenticity at bay through our fear of being found out. Authenticity becomes real when we admit our frustrations, acknowledge our weaknesses, and disclose our insecurities. We are never real until we open our wounded hearts. Everyone's heart has been wounded, but most of us would rather protect our wounds than divulge them. That's why we wear masks and stifle our true feelings.

No one has written more sensitively on the gift of vulnerability than Henri Nouwen in his book *The Wounded Healer*. He points out that "making one's own wounds a source of healing . . . does not call for a sharing of superficial personal pains but for a constant willingness to see one's own pain and suffering as rising from the depth of the human condition."

And that's precisely what allows us to speak the truth in love. Jesus didn't speak the truth from a self-centered heart. He did it from within the context of pain for anyone who is missing the true message of God. His conviction was so powerful that he couldn't care less what others thought. His truth-telling came from a deep and personal anguish for those who were hung up on superficiality, externals, and hypocrisy. He spoke truth to save them from themselves. He spoke truth from love.

When we separate love from truth-telling, we are trading genuineness for approval. We are trading boldness for cowardice. This creates a false and fleeting connection at best—about an inch deep. But when we risk rejection and get real, we begin to love more like Jesus.

> **As scarce as truth is, the supply has always been in excess of the demand.**
>
> —Josh Billings

To Ponder

- One of the most compelling stories in the New Testament occurs when Jesus becomes angry in the temple. What do you make of it after reading this chapter? What was his motive, and why did he become so emotional?
- We all fear rejection at some level. That's why we

wear interpersonal masks (presenting an image that's not congruent with how we really are). What's your go-to mask when you shy away from truth-telling? Do you wear the "pleasant" mask? The "brush it off with humor" mask? What's your inclination?

- Jesus says we need to speak the truth, but with love: "Confront him with the need for repentance, and offer again God's forgiving love." How have you done this in your own relationships? What's your biggest personal challenge in doing so?

- To be a better truth-teller, a bold person in your relationships, you have to be willing to risk rejection. How would you rate yourself on this ability? What's one practical way for you to improve in this area? Is there a relationship right now that needs your attention in this way?

- Jesus held such powerful convictions that when he spoke out against injustice or hypocrisy, he couldn't care less what others thought of him. Have you ever felt that way? When and why? Were you able to do it from a heart of sincere love?

CHAPTER 5

SELF-GIVING

*Whoever finds their life will lose it, and
whoever loses their life for my sake will find it.*
—Jesus

I've got to be honest. I've been putting off this chapter. I debated even telling you. After all, you'd never know it. The book has five chapters, and they're all here between two covers, regardless. But I think you deserve to know. I've been putting off writing this chapter for months. The rest of the book has been done. It's been written and reviewed. My publisher gave the other chapters the green light. My editor carefully reviewed them. But not this one. This one has been waiting.

Why? Two reasons.

First, I knew it meant facing my own selfishness head-on. And who wants that? I'm pretty content ignoring my self-serving ways. In fact, like most people, I'm a master at denying them. I like the idea that it's other people who need to be less selfish, but *moi*? I knew this chapter would mean I'd have to excavate my selfishness and own it. In an article titled "I'm O.K., You're Selfish," *New York Times Magazine* reported only 17 percent of people say they are selfish themselves, but 60 percent think that most other people are selfish most of the time. Denial, anyone?

Second, I've struggled to make sense of this whole idea. Of all the ideas Jesus had about loving others, this idea of self-giving has been the toughest one for me to understand. Don't get me wrong. I knew from the start it had to be included in the book. It's a hallmark of how Jesus taught us to love. And I understand the concept and what it means. But I've struggled to understand how you can really do it. How can you possibly surrender your self-focus? More important, why? Why would any rational human being want to ignore self-interest and give up pursuing the things they desire most? Why would anyone give up their own needs, drives, rights, and goals? Isn't that the best way to be happy and fulfilled?

Both of these reasons for putting off this chapter fell apart when I discovered a surprising line of research that reveals just how incredibly rewarding and fulfilling it is to own our self-serving ways and start living an unselfish life. Turns out I've had it all backward. You don't sacrifice fulfillment by giving up your life—you find it. It's exactly what Jesus said: when you lose your life in love, you find it.

Consider psychologist Bernard Rimland. He earned his PhD at Pennsylvania State University, and his career was on a fast track. But three years later, in 1956, he hit a bump in the road. His son, Mark, was born and diagnosed with what was then a little known disorder called autism. In fact, at the time, Rimland, like most, had never heard of the term.

> **Our greatest fulfillment lies in giving ourselves to others.**
>
> —Henri J. M. Nouwen

That began a quest for Rimland to understand autism. He devoted much of his career to it, writing one of the first books on the topic and in 1967 establishing the Autism Research Institute. But along the way, Rimland did a simple experiment that sheds some light on one of the great paradoxical truths of the ages: to find your life, you must lose it.

He asked 216 students to list the initials of ten people they knew best, yielding a grand list of some two thousand people. He then asked them to indicate whether each person seemed happy or not. Finally, he asked them to go over each name again, indicating if the person seemed selfish or unselfish. In other words, were they mostly interested in their own desires or were they willing to be inconvenienced by others and their desires?

The striking result: 70 percent of those judged unselfish seemed happy while 95 percent of those judged selfish seemed *un*happy. Rimland was surprised by the paradox: "Selfish people are, by definition, those whose activities are devoted to *bringing themselves happiness*. Yet, at least as judged by others, these selfish people are far less likely to be happy than those whose efforts are devoted to making others happy."

This finding begins to get at that saying Jesus repeated more than any other: "Whoever finds his life will lose it, and whoever loses his life for my sake will find it." It flips our intuitive sense of self-interest inside out. It also gets at why Jesus was radical about learning to give ourselves to others.

The Self-Giving of Jesus

Like everyone else, I can remember precisely where I was on the morning of September 11, 2001, when I learned of the terror attack on the World Trade Center in New York. I was sitting on the edge of a bed in a hotel room in Oklahoma City. My wife, Leslie, and I were preparing to speak in a convocation at the only historically black college in the state, Langston University. The news of the attack on the television that morning, of course, changed everything. I'll never forget it.

Chances are, if you're old enough, you won't either. Some experiences are so jolting, unexpected, remarkable, and surprising that they become seared into our memory banks forever. Memory specialists call them *hot spots* or *flashbulb memories*. The surprise of something we didn't expect or something so incredibly meaningful (like proposing marriage) releases a chemical in our brain called glutamate. It improves our mental processing in the moment and focuses our attention in powerful ways—making the memory clear, vivid, detailed, and enduring. Flashbulb memories include richer sensory detail than others. The neural chemical in our brain cements the memory in place, as it were, making it nearly impossible to forget.

Not only do flashbulb memories become something we can easily recall, they shape the way we behave going forward. In fact, experts consider recollections as mental time travel—not just about the past but also a version of the future. A growing body of research at Harvard University suggests that the purpose of memory is far more extensive than simply helping us

You will find as
you look back
upon your life
that the moments
when you have
truly lived are the
moments when
you have done
things in the
spirit of love.

—Henry Drummond

store and recall information about what has already happened. For example, researchers have shown how memory helps us draw a mental sketch of someone's personality and imagine how that person might behave in a future social situation. In other words, recollecting a past event gives us a clearer imagination of how we will behave in the future. The things we remember change who we are and who we are becoming. Our habits, ideas, and hopes—even our promptings to love—are influenced by what we remember.

Jesus didn't need modern research to leverage this fact. On the last evening of his life, he was deliberate in creating an indelible memory that shaped the future of humankind: he hosts a final meal with his disciples in Jerusalem. It's held on the second floor of a building near the Pool of Siloam around a long rectangular table just eighteen inches tall. Pillows surround the table where the disciples and Jesus can lounge in the traditional fashion.

Once in the room and around the low table, Jesus does something unprecedented and carefully calibrated. He ensured that it would be a flashbulb memory burned into the mind of each disciple and passed along to future generations who would follow. This was no accident. Jesus planned his actions. It was premeditated. He wanted this meal to be remembered and celebrated. Jesus, in fact, said it straight out that evening: "Do this in remembrance of me."

Before the meal of bread and wine and Jesus' accompanying message of profound symbolism, he humbles himself in a way that shocked his disciples. He does something so incongruent to what they were expecting and so deeply meaningful that it was guaranteed to stick in their memory forever. Their teacher, their Lord, takes a towel and basin and begins carefully washing each man's feet with water. The disciples are stunned. Dismayed. Overwhelmed. This task was normally reserved for lowly servants. But here is their venerated rabbi kneeling before each of them, one after the other, to lovingly rinse the road dust from their feet.

It's an inversion. It's upside down and doesn't make sense. Power and recognition are on the minds of the disciples, and Jesus is demonstrating service and sacrifice. He knows each of them well: the boisterous James and John whom he called "sons of thunder," Simon the zealot whose passion for politics could be easily provoked, the skeptical Thomas who struggled with doubts, upbeat Andrew, rash-tongued Peter, and all the rest. Jesus even washes the feet of Judas, whom he knows is about to betray him. Jesus looks each

> **What a grand thing, to be loved! What a grander thing still, to love!**
>
> —Victor Hugo

of these men in the eyes, considers their personalities, and displays uncompromising humility. He doesn't pay someone to wash their feet; Jesus does it himself. He becomes a lowly, unpretentious, self-giving servant.

It's easy to miss the profundity of this act because of the gulf in time and culture between us and that fateful evening. A modern-day equivalent might be your pastor coming to your home to wash your dirty dishes or clean your bathrooms. Or maybe the governor of your state stopping by to sweep out your garage or separate your garbage. The analogies lack the personal and intimate experience of what Jesus did, but they get at the startling act of humility and service. The self-giving act of their rabbi surely endeared the disciples to him more than ever.

Of course, what Jesus did was more than an act of affection. It's a life lesson. Jesus tells the disciples they must follow his example with each other. They must become like servants, setting aside concern for position and privilege. They must place others above themselves. Through foot washing, Jesus unforgettably shows that service, not status, is what he's about: "The Son of Man did not come to be served, but to serve."

Even before that last night, Jesus spoke to his followers about this radical servant attitude. When they originally joined Jesus and his movement, three years earlier, they were focused on reaping rewards. They

Make the most of every opportunity you have for doing good.

—Ephesians 5:16 TLB

wanted a payoff for leaving their lives and following him. They quarreled over who would get what role. Two of them even had their mother make a special request to Jesus on their behalf, ensuring they'd be promoted. A constant power grab entwined the twelve.

Jesus told them repeatedly that power games were fundamentally alien to life inside God's kingdom. It's not about being first or more prominent. It's about heartfelt service. It's about love. But even up to the time of their final dinner together they were jockeying for position and squabbling over who was greatest. So Jesus leaves them—and us—with an indelible act that spoke in ways words cannot. He leaves us on the last night of his life with an unforgettable act of humble service that sums up, perhaps more than anything else he did short of the cross, what it means to love like Jesus.

Self-Giving

adjective
self-giv•ing \self-'gi-ving\

Self-giving is selfishness in reverse. It is not concerned with benefits, and it expects nothing in return. Whether it is offering directions to someone who appears lost, giving an especially generous tip to a server who seems needy, or encouraging a friend who didn't get an expected promotion, self-giving love is done out of care, compassion, and kindness—expecting neither repayment nor appreciation.

It comes down to motive. You can be a giver and still expect something in return. We call it giving "with strings attached." In other words, there is an expectation connected to the giving. The origin of the idiom "no strings attached" is directly tied to eighteenth-century fabric merchants who would mark flaws in woven cloth by tying small strings to the bottom of the bolts at the locations where flaws were present. When a tailor or dressmaker needed flawless cloth, he or she would ask the merchant to provide fabric "with no strings attached." The custom persists today. And so does the practice of giving with an expectation that we'll be getting something in return. True self-giving involves no "this for that," no quid pro quo. True self-giving is offering the best of who you are to others, and it comes with no strings attached.

What Keeps Us from Being Self-Giving?

One day a student asked famed anthropologist Margaret Mead for the earliest sign of civilization in a given culture. He expected the answer to be a clay pot or perhaps a fishhook or grinding stone. Her answer was "a healed femur."

Mead explained that no healed femurs are found where the law of the jungle, survival of the fittest, reigns. A healed femur shows that someone cared. Someone had to do that injured person's hunting and gathering until the leg healed. The evidence of compassion, said Mead, is the first sign of civilization.

It's also the first sign of self-giving love. And the greatest barrier to compassion is fear. The fear of not being first—of not getting what we need or what we want— pushes us to the front. It causes us to seek our own advantage and look past what might help others.

Countless studies back this up. Consider one published in the journal *World Development*. Researchers asked people in rural Colombia to play a game in which they had to decide how much firewood to take from a forest, with the consideration that deforestation would result in poor water quality. This game was analogous to real life for the people of the village. In some cases, people played the games in small groups but couldn't communicate about their decisions with players outside their group. In other cases, they could communicate with players outside their group. In a third condition, the players couldn't communicate but were given rules specifying how much firewood they could gather.

Love, and do what you will.

—St. Augustine

When allowed to communicate, the people in the small groups set aside self-interest and gathered less firewood for themselves, preserving water quality in the forest for the larger group as a whole. Regulations and incentives, on the other hand, had a negative result over time: People gradually began to gather more and more firewood for themselves, risking a fine but ultimately putting their self-interest first. Why? Fear of missing out on what they needed and wanted.

Dozens of studies show that if you offer someone money to perform a task that they would otherwise happily do without pay, it turns on the "What's in it for me?" way of thinking. So much so that they will become more and more focused on their own self-interest (getting time off, getting paid more, and so on). It's in our nature to look out for ourselves. And while situational factors, like getting paid, can push people toward self-interest, all of us—regardless of our circumstances—can break the instinctual habit of routinely putting our own interests first. We can overcome our fear of missing out on what we need or want. If we want to love like Jesus, we've got to get a lock on placing other people's needs ahead of our own. Fortunately, in his teaching, Jesus gives us a clear-cut path for doing just that.

How Self-Giving Are You?

If you're curious to get a little snapshot of how inclined you currently are to practice mindfulness in order to love others well, take a moment to honestly indicate how frequently you experienced each of the following over the past week. You can complete your self-test online at LoveLikeThatBook.com and receive a summary of your progress along the way.

I'm intentional about putting myself in other people's shoes to imagine how they think and feel.

Never	Rarely	Sometimes	Often	Very Often

I work hard to treat other people the way I want to be treated.

Never	Rarely	Sometimes	Often	Very Often

I'm known by my friends as someone who puts others' needs ahead of my own.

Never	Rarely	Sometimes	Often	Very Often

I listen intently to others and intentionally put away my phone or other distractions to give them full focus.

Never	Rarely	Sometimes	Often	Very Often

**I work at emptying myself of a selfish
desire to change other people.**

Never	Rarely	Sometimes	Often	Very Often

I love others as I love myself.

Never	Rarely	Sometimes	Often	Very Often

I'm happy to play second fiddle.

Never	Rarely	Sometimes	Often	Very Often

I go the extra mile for other people.

Never	Rarely	Sometimes	Often	Very Often

I'm generous toward people in my life.

Never	Rarely	Sometimes	Often	Very Often

**I'm willing to put myself second in
order to put another person first.**

Never	Rarely	Sometimes	Often	Very Often

Now take a moment to review these items. If most of your answers are "often" and "very often," you're well on your way to being self-giving. You're more willing than most to set aside self-interest to meet the needs of others. If, on the other hand, most of your answers are "never" and "rarely," you will benefit significantly from Jesus' teaching on emptying yourself to better meet the needs of others.

What Jesus Taught Us About Being Self-Giving

On September 18, 2007, Randy Pausch gave a lecture, his "last lecture," at Carnegie Mellon, titled "Really Achieving Your Childhood Dreams." The talk was modeled after an ongoing series of lectures where top academics are asked to think deeply about what matters to them and give a hypothetical "final talk" on it.

For Pausch it wasn't hypothetical. He'd been diagnosed with terminal cancer and knew his time was limited. When he stepped to the lectern, he received a long standing ovation from over four hundred colleagues and students who had gathered to hear him talk about the most important message he had to deliver.

If Jesus was to give his "last lecture" on what really matters most in our relationships, I think it would have been all about self-giving love. He spoke about it repeatedly with incredible clarity. In the Sermon on the Mount, he used a memorable illustration that continues to inspire people who don't even know where it

We make

a living by

what we get.

We make a

life by what

we give.

—Unknown

came from—including customer-service specialists at places like Nordstrom and Amazon.

During the time of Jesus, the Roman Empire established a law requiring boys in villages to carry Roman soldiers' backpacks one mile from their home. It gave soldiers a rest from hauling all their gear. The practice was so pervasive that most kids would measure a mile down the road in both directions from their house and drive a stake in the ground to mark the distance. That way they knew exactly how far they would need to carry a soldier's pack. It was unfair, inconvenient, and often backbreaking. But it was the law. And those stakes in the ground represented the minimum requirement to fulfill it.

As Jesus preached his sermon to a crowd overlooking the Sea of Galilee, he used this Roman practice as an illustration for how to improve relationships. It was revolutionary. Unheard of. Jesus said: "If someone forces you to go one mile, go with him two miles." He was saying that if you want to be self-giving, this is how you do it. You do what others don't expect. And by doing more than is required, you are automatically setting your self-interest aside. You are putting your own needs in abeyance. You are living unselfishly. Guaranteed.

Sometimes you hear people use the phrase as a motivational slogan in business or athletics. In fact, it's almost a cliché. A coach wants you to "go the extra mile" in your workout at the gym. Fine. But that's not what Jesus was talking about. The extra mile, as Jesus taught, was about doing more for others than anyone would expect.

In that same sermon, Jesus gave another practical way of being self-giving. And it's just as radical. But it's so brief and so brilliant even atheists know it. It's been referred to as the ultimate formula for successful relationships. We all call it the golden rule. Jesus never called it that, and the Bible doesn't give it that name. But the idea Jesus articulated is so important and is such a good summary of unselfishness that it was given the name "the golden rule" by Bible translators in the sixteenth and seventeenth centuries, using a popular saying at that time.

Jesus said: "Ask yourself what you want people to do for you, then grab the initiative and do it for *them*!" Or as a more classic translation puts it:

"Do to others as you would have them do to you."

On another occasion, Jesus made it even more succinct:

"Love your neighbor as yourself."

Enough said, right? It comes down to actively treating others the way we want to be treated. It's how we leverage our natural

> No one has ever become poor by giving.
>
> —Anne Frank

self-interest to fuel love for others. It's genius. We all want respect, appreciation, grace, understanding, patience, and kindness from others. Well, then that's what we are to actively give others.

Bible scholars note that the golden rule is proactive. It's positive. Other religions, including Confucianism, Hinduism, and Buddhism contain similar commands:

- Confucianism: "What you do not want done to yourself, do not do to others."
- Hinduism: "This is the sum of duty: do not do to others what would cause pain if done to you."
- Buddhism: "Hurt not others in ways that you yourself would find hurtful."

All of these, in contrast to what Jesus said, are negative. They may seem to be saying the same thing as Jesus' golden rule, but they are actually a negative opposite. It's referred to as the "ethic of reciprocity." They are focused on prohibiting unfair treatment. The idea is that you should not do something to another person if you know it would cause them pain. In other words, if something would cause you pain, it will cause them pain, so don't do it to them. But this "silver rule," as it is sometimes called, requires nothing of you. It requires no love, no positive action. You can be completely apathetic in your relationships and still follow the silver rule.

But this is not the case with Jesus. The golden rule that Jesus taught, in contrast, goes beyond reciprocity. It is not passive. It requires proactive behavior—doing something that benefits others. It requires initiative. It requires empathy.

How to Be More Self-Giving

I can answer this question of how to be more self-giving in a single phrase: Put yourself in another's shoes. Or better yet, a single word: empathy.

I've been studying empathy for nearly three decades. I started in graduate school, writing my doctoral dissertation on the topic. And all these years later empathy still fascinates me. I think it's the single most important relationship skill set we have.

> Love is, above all, the gift of oneself.
>
> —Jean Anouilh

When teaching my counseling students at the university, I use a simple metaphor to make the distinction between sympathy and empathy. I tell them that sympathy is standing on the shore and throwing a life ring out to a person who is struggling in the water. Every decent human being would do this. It flows with our adrenaline.

Empathy is much riskier. Empathy is diving into the water and thrashing around in the cold waves with that person to bring them to safety. Not everyone does that. In fact, it's so rare that we call these people "heroes."

And it's just as heroic when we do this in our relationships. Why? Because empathy *is* risky. It will change you. Once you immerse yourself in someone else's predicament or situation, you won't look at him or her the same way. You'll have a new perspective that makes you more patient, more grace-giving, more caring, and more loving.

By the way, you might be thinking that since I've spent the better part of my life researching empathy that I'd have a lock on it in my own relationships. Think again. I'm in full agreement with whoever said, "Trying to observe the slow shift from self-centeredness to empathy is like trying to watch grass grow."

Empathy is a process. It's an art we learn over a lifetime. You can't check it off your to-do list, but you can get better at it. And one of the best ways I've discovered for getting better at empathy came from an encounter I had with the famous psychiatrist and bestselling author of *The Road Less Traveled*, Scott Peck. I spent three days with him and a small group of people in Knoxville, Tennessee, to explore the struggle we humans have with our egos. And from our time together, I'll never forget his simple strategy. After various exercises and interactions within our group of a dozen or so people, Peck said, "I want to show you what enables us to see beyond our self-interest and really empathize." He called it *emptiness*.

He was talking about the capacity we have to empty ourselves of our need for other people to do what we want. Let's face it—we are often obsessed with demanding that life go the way we want it to go. We can spend weeks, sometimes years, in a perpetual stew because something did not go as we wished—or because someone messed us up. We fuss and fume. But when we empty ourselves of this compulsive need to have our own way—when we lose our life, as it were—something almost mystical takes place deep within our soul. We find our life.

> He who does
> not love does
> not know
> God; for
> God is love.
>
> —1 John 4:8 RSV

When we hold our desires loosely, a massive burden is released and a new happiness is found. It's what philosopher and Roman emperor Marcus Aurelius was getting at when he said, "To live happily is an inward power of the soul." When we surrender our selfishness, we are no longer limited to defining our happiness by merely getting what we want. Emptying ourselves of the burden to always get our way frees our soul and opens the way to understanding others. It opens the door for empathy.

Okay. So I can almost hear you asking: Does this mean that to be emptied of self-serving ways we must give up our needs, drives, rights, and goals? It's an important question, and I want to be clear: the love that comes from being emptied of self-seeking ways is not necessarily about self-denial. I have seen many well-intentioned people set out to "love" others by denying their own needs—as if performing a sacrifice was the goal.

It's not.

Being emptied of self-seeking desires is not about doing without. As the greatest of love poems makes clear, we can give our body to be burned and still not be loving. Self-giving love does not demand a huge sacrifice. Small things, done with great love, most often characterize the actions of a person who has found the power of self-giving. But sometimes we must admit that even the smallest of sacrifices is hard to come by.

Leonard Bernstein, the famous orchestra conductor, was asked, "What is the most difficult instrument to play?" He responded with quick wit: "Second fiddle. I can get plenty of first violinists, but to find one who plays second violin with as much enthusiasm, now that's a problem." The apostle Paul understood the same challenge when he wrote his letter to the Romans: "Love from the center of who you are. . . . Be good friends who love deeply; practice playing second fiddle."

So here's the question: Are you willing to put yourself second in order to put another person first? Are you willing to be changed? I want to say it again: once you empathize with another, you become a different person—maybe slightly, maybe significantly. But be assured, you change. You don't look at that person— whether it be a friend, your spouse, your child, a coworker, or a total stranger—the same way again. Every act of accurate empathy is like a little carving from a sculptor's chisel, causing you to have a slightly new perspective. It can't be helped. When you imagine what life must be like in the other person's skin, you change. Empathy shapes you. It fashions a heart that is more closely aligned with Jesus.

To Ponder

- What do you make of the survey showing that only 17 percent of us say we are selfish but we see most other people as being selfish most of the time? Do you admit you are a selfish person at least some of the time? Why or why not? Are you

"If you walk around with your nose in the air, you're going to end up flat on your face. But if you're content to be simply yourself, you will become more than yourself."

—Jesus

more self-focused or less self-focused than most other people you know?

- Imagine being in the upper room with Jesus and the disciples for the Last Supper. Jesus, your teacher, begins to carefully wash your feet with water. Put yourself in that day and age with all the meaning this custom would have. How are you feeling and why? What flashbulb memory would you take with you from that experience?

- Do you agree that the greatest barrier to compassion is fear—the fear of not being first, of not getting what you want? Can you recount a concrete example of this from your own life? What does it teach you?

- When Jesus taught the principle of going the extra mile it was—and still is—radical. Do you aspire to do that in your relationships? Why or why not? When was the last time you were intentional about walking the extra mile for someone? What happened?

- How are you doing when it comes to putting yourself in other people's shoes? Would you give yourself good marks for empathy? Why? Can you think of a specific example from the past week where you were intentional about seeing the world—or at least a particular issue—from someone else's perspective?

HOW IS THIS EVEN POSSIBLE?

I am the Vine, you are the branches.
—Jesus

I've been meeting with these guys for a decade. Ten hard-charging, time-starved men who didn't really know each other at the start. But we all knew we wanted to live a better life—we wanted to be better people. So we gathered for the first time in the boardroom of a high-rise office building in downtown Seattle. We called it "the 5 Percent Club" because we wanted to focus on the 5 percent of our lives we don't broadcast to other people. The good, the bad, and the ugly.

We don't study books. We don't have a curriculum or watch TED Talks. We don't even give each other advice (we actually have a rule against it). We have no agenda other than talking about what's on our minds that we haven't talked about with others. We ask each other questions. And we listen. We do this for two hours every other Tuesday. And we've been doing this for ten years.

Think we know each other pretty well by now? You bet. That's why when I recently asked the group a question and they didn't have much to say, I didn't have any problem pushing them for an honest answer.

Here's the question I posed: "Who do you hate?"

Nobody answered. They sat in silence as the question hung in midair for several beats. Then, finally, one guy spoke up: "I don't hate anyone." Others quickly nodded in agreement. "Me too," they each muttered.

"Okay," I said, "then let me ask another question: Who has messed up the trajectory of your life?"

They weren't so quiet now. In fact, the room became electric. Everyone seemed to have a near ready-made list of people who had made their life difficult. "Pete in St. Louis," (not his real name or the real city) one guy said. "If it weren't for him, I would have been promoted and I'd be at a very different place today." As he continued to talk about Pete, he contorted his face to mimic the way Pete talked. Some of us laughed.

Some grimaced. After many years, the thought of Pete evoked painful emotions in our friend. It was obvious.

Somebody else spoke up. "There was this guy at my old firm, and he's probably the main reason I left. I can't stand to even mention his name." Then someone else chimed in. Then another. Of course, I brought up a person who complicated my life too.

Without any suggestion or direction, each of us had made a literal list of people who had complicated our lives—people who made us angry. We each had a list of people we loathed, disliked, detested—okay, hated. We had to admit it.

Why the question? Because I'd read this puzzling passage and was curious to know what my friends thought of it: "If anyone boasts, 'I love God,' and goes right on hating his brother or sister, thinking nothing of it, he is a liar. If he won't love the person he can see, how can he love the God he can't see? The command we have from Christ is blunt: Loving God includes loving people. You've got to love both."

So now this group of ten men—all God-loving followers of Jesus—realized that we had a problem. We realized we had people in our lives we actually hated. Some of us even confessed that we wouldn't be heartsick if something bad happened to these people. That's when one of us spoke up: "Is it even possible to love like Jesus did?"

Maybe you've been asking the same question as you've been reading this book. You might be wondering if the incredibly high bar of love is obtainable in the gritty real-life world of relationships.

I've pointed to five concrete ways to help us love more like Jesus:

1. Be mindful—not indifferent—by seeing what others don't.
2. Be approachable—not exclusive—by moving out of your comfort zone.
3. Be grace-full—not judgmental—by not limiting your love to people who deserve it.
4. Be bold—not fearful—by speaking truthfully and risking rejection.
5. Be self-giving—not self-serving—by emptying yourself for empathy.

I want you to review this list and ask yourself which of these behaviors comes easiest for you. Which is toughest? Now let's move from the abstract to the concrete. Consider your personal relationships. Who in your life is the toughest to love? I'm not forcing you into admitting you hate anyone. I just want you to think about the person who isn't easy to love.

Here's the test: Can you love this person like Jesus loves them? Can you love them in ways that are not cautious but extravagant? Can you give them grace? Can you love them not in order to get something from them but to give yourself to them? Can you love like that?

I'll tell you straight up. I can't. It feels impossible. Unnatural. So, if you are saying "I can't love like that either," I'm with you.

But here's what I've learned. Ultimately, loving like Jesus—loving at this incredibly high level—is an internal quest. It's not so much about *doing* as it is about *being*.

Sure, we can work to focus our attention and strive to be more mindful of others. We can lower our guard and open our hearts to be more approachable and less exclusive. We can curb our criticism and be more graceful. We can risk rejection to forge a more authentic relationship. We can even sacrifice our self-interest to play second fiddle. But ultimately, on our own, striving to do loving things, we will fail miserably.

There is only one way for any of us to resolve the tension between the high ideals Jesus taught us and the harsh reality of our self-serving lives: to accept that we will never measure up to the high standard of loving like Jesus, and we don't have to.

We don't have to because Jesus wants to do the loving through us. Our only task is to allow this to happen. This is the most important truth you will take away from this book. Let me say it again: the long and the short of it is that we love like Jesus when we allow Jesus to *love through us*. It's not about our effort. We are not trying to imitate Jesus. It's an inside job. It's about being a channel for his love.

If you're feeling skeptical all of a sudden, I get that. This sounds perplexing if not mystical. That's because it is. Previously I borrowed a line from French physicist Blaise Pascal, "We know truth, not only by the reason, but also by the heart." So as you consider how Christ can live within us, I ask you to reason with your heart as well as your head.

The mystery of this notion is resolved, in part, through experience. Millions upon millions of Christians over the centuries can testify that when you are a true God-follower, attuned to his Spirit, Christ lives in you. He abides in you. The apostle Paul confesses his struggle to love like Jesus and eventually said it this way in his letter to the Galatians:

> I tried keeping rules and working my head off to please God, and it didn't work. So, I quit being a "law man" so that I could be *God's* man. Christ's life showed me how, and enabled me to do it. I identified myself completely with him. Indeed, I have been crucified with Christ. My ego is no longer central. It is no longer important that I appear righteous

before you or have your good opinion, and I am no longer driven to impress God. Christ lives in me. The life you see me living is not "mine," but it is lived by faith in the Son of God, who loved me and gave himself for me. I am not going to go back on that.

Paul is revealing the secret to this mystery of how we can actually love more and more like Jesus. In his letter to the Jesus-followers in Colossians, he writes: "This mystery has been kept in the dark for a long time, but now it's out in the open. . . . The mystery in a nutshell is just this: Christ is in you, so therefore you can look forward to sharing in God's glory. It's that simple."

No other religion or movement implies that the living presence of its founder lives in its followers. Muhammad does not indwell Muslims. Buddha does not inhabit Buddhists. But Christ's followers embrace the promise: Christ lives in you. "You'll be changed from the inside out." When we invite Jesus to live in us, His Spirit can bring the best out of us.

The Spirit of Jesus that lives in us is not out of reach. It doesn't require any bizarre spiritual practices. You don't have to sacrifice an animal, seek out a shaman or a prophet; no need to isolate yourself in a barren desert or do a serious fast; no requirement to wear certain kind of clothes or practice self-flagellation; no need to even go on a simple spiritual retreat. No religious ritual needed. We simply invite the Spirit of Christ to live in us. Scripture calls it the Holy Spirit.

Jesus himself calls it the Friend:

> But when the Friend comes, the Spirit of the Truth, he will take you by the hand and guide you into all the truth there is. He won't draw attention to himself, but will make sense out of what is about to happen and, indeed, out of all that I have done and said.

The Holy Spirit is not a vague, ethereal, or shadowy force. The Holy Spirit is a Friend—the best kind of Friend—who walks with us, helping us live and love at the highest levels. And who wouldn't want a friend who does that?

Every social scientist knows the value of a good friend. Study after study reveals that a good friend who wants the best for us—someone we respect and trust—empowers us to be better. Toni Antonucci, a professor of psychology at the University of Michigan, developed a structure of friendship represented by three concentric circles that she describes as very close, close, and not-so-close but still meaningful personal ties. The rings can play different roles, with strong and emotional ties serving some functions and less intimate friendships filling other needs.

But it's the center circle where we find our most significant relationships, our closest friends who fill an invaluable role as confidant, someone who listens and pays attention, someone who is willing to help when others aren't. Someone who is invested in us being the best we can be. These are the connections that shape our character and help us cultivate compassion. Aristotle had a name for these inner-circle relationships: "friendships based on character." He said they were instrumental in our moral development. Our close friends, according to Aristotle, shape our character. They come alongside us, for example, and help us realize that the generous action we just made is in fact generous and not wasteful. They help us leverage our strengths and improve upon our weaknesses. As iron sharpens iron, they help us become our best selves.

And that's what Jesus is saying about our ultimate Friend, the Holy Spirit. At the very heart of our friendship circle is the Comforter and Counselor who is advocating for us to be better than the person we are tempted to settle for.

In fact, Scripture gives us several names for the Holy Spirit, and when we look at the five ways to love like Jesus that I've noted in this book, it's interesting to see how Scripture has a name for the Holy Spirit that aligns with each one:

1. Be mindful—by leaning into the "Spirit of Knowledge."
2. Be approachable—by leaning into the "Spirit of Comfort."
3. Be grace-full—by leaning into the "Spirit of Grace."
4. Be bold—by leaning into the "Spirit of Might."
5. Be self-giving—by leaning into the "Spirit of God."

The key to all of this is in the "leaning"—the conscious intention of inviting and receiving the Spirit in our lives, moment by moment. In my experience, the Holy Spirit doesn't mystically come into your life with a slap on the forehead to instantly improve everything about you, ensuring your happiness. The Spirit-filled life doesn't eliminate struggle. Being filled with the Spirit doesn't exempt us from pain. Walking in the Spirit is something we do *in* the pain and struggle, not *instead* of the pain and struggle.

The Spirit-filled life is a supernatural life, for sure. But it requires us to do our part too. We don't just "let go and let God." We still need to step out in faith. We have to risk. We have to open up, reach out, repent, worship, fellowship, obey, and do all the other things a life of genuine faith entails. But keep in mind that as we do these things, we don't do them alone. We don't even do them by our own willpower. We partner with the Spirit. Our Friend falls in step with us, and we fall in step with him. We work together.

How the Holy Spirit Works

Someone said that many of us think that the Holy Spirit is like our pituitary gland. We know it's there, we're glad we've got it, and we don't want to lose it, but we're not exactly sure what it does. Well, the Holy Spirit does a lot. For our purposes, the Holy Spirit is our teacher, guide, reminder, comforter, and enabler. The Spirit is not a mysterious force; the Spirit is the presence of God living in us. The Spirit is our Friend.

Some have summarized the partnership of the Father, Son, and Holy Spirit this way: *the Father plans, the Son accomplishes, and the Spirit applies.* Theologians may debate the simplicity of this idea, but the point I'm making with it is that the Spirit leaves fingerprints on our loving actions. The Spirit attunes us to love in ways we might never consider on our own. The Spirit is what enabled Jesus to see Zacchaeus in ways that others didn't. The Spirit helped Jesus become approachable to outcasts like Mary Magdalene. The Spirit empowered Jesus to offer grace to a woman caught red-handed in the act of adultery. The Spirit emboldened Jesus to expose the motives of false teachers and legalistic leaders of his day. And it was the Spirit who comforted Jesus in his final days so that he could flip the script and show his disciples how to serve rather than be served as they shared a final meal together. In short, it was the Spirit who helped Jesus intuit how to love others at every step.

That's how the Spirit works.

When leaning into the Spirit becomes a habit, the gray matter in our brain quiets down and love begins to work on autopilot. We loosen up our minds from working overtime trying to weigh the scales of our efforts to love or not to love. It's no longer a question. Life in the Spirit means the decision is already made. No more analysis paralysis. Tension eases as spiritual intuition increases. *When you clear your head—when you still your rational mind enough to make room for the Spirit to work in your intuitive mind—love recalibrates our agendas and pushes pride aside to make room for love at the highest levels.*

In my experience, the Spirit often works through intuition—that effortless, immediate, unreasoned sense of truth. Skilled decision makers know that they can depend on their intuition, but at the same time they may feel uncomfortable trusting a source of power that seems so unintended or maybe even ethereal. It's tough to lean into our intuition without our rational mind, just as it may be a struggle to think our way to living life in the Spirit. Maybe that's why French physicist Blaise Pascal said, "The heart has its reasons, which reason does not know."

Some people think of intuition as an inborn trait that some people get and others don't. But not scientists. They don't see just some people as being blessed with intuition. They say all of us hold an intuitive capacity. They say intuition grows within *all* of us. Everyone can access this part of themselves.

Those who say they lack intuition are essentially relying exclusively on their rational mind. Psychologist Antoine Bechara at the University of Southern California studied brain-damaged patients who could not form emotional intuitions when making a decision. They were left to decide purely via deliberate reasoning. "They ended up doing such a complicated analysis, factoring everything in, that it could take them hours to decide between two kinds of cereal," the researchers said.

Let's face it, our intuition is a gift. Albert Einstein called it a sacred gift. And it just may be one of the prime places to discover God's Spirit. When Einstein labeled the intuitive mind as "the sacred gift," he was commenting on its spiritual implications. To ignore the spiritual profundity of the insightful whispers we hear in our intuitive mind is to miss out on their potential power.

But is Einstein right? Could it be that divine guidance actually comes to us through our intuitive mind? Could those unreasoned moments be heavenly whispers from the Spirit?

•

I've talked with many people of faith, sincere churchgoing Christians who are doing their best to follow God's principles, but they are missing out on life in the Spirit. They aren't living a supernatural life simply because they are either trying to do it on their own terms, through their own effort—so they end up comparing their progress to others (giving self-righteousness an open door)—or they've never truly understood that all they need to do is ask our Friend to help them. In the upside-down economy of loving like Jesus, it starts with seeking and knocking rather than striving and exerting.

Paul taught this lesson several times, especially in his letters to the Galatians and the Ephesians. He said, "Let us keep in step with the Spirit." And he was quick to note that it does no good to compare ourselves to others in this area:

> Since this is the kind of life we have chosen, the life
> of the Spirit, let us make sure that we do not just
> hold it as an idea in our heads or a sentiment in our

hearts, but work out its implications in every detail of our lives.

In other words, he's saying we need to be intentional. In all aspects of our lives, at home, at work and even with strangers, we need to lean into the Holy Spirit. And he continues by underscoring how each of us does this in our own way:

That means we will not compare ourselves with each other as if one of us were better and another worse. We have far more interesting things to do with our lives. Each of us is an original.

So don't get caught up in measuring your progress against others. Instead, get immersed in knowing how to fall in step with the Spirit. And if you're not sure where to begin in this process, consider the five ways to love like Jesus that we've covered in this book. They just may be five of the best ways to walk in the Spirit of Christ:

1. We need to *open our eyes* to become mindful of the Spirit in our lives. We need to pray: "Help me recognize you and learn your voice. I want to see you, moment by moment, in my life." Here's what Jesus said about this:

"If you love me, show it by doing what I've told you. I will talk to the Father, and he'll provide you another Friend so that you will always have someone with you. This Friend is the Spirit of Truth. The godless world can't take him in because it doesn't have eyes to see him, doesn't know what to look for. But you know him already because he has been staying with you, and will even be *in* you!"

2. We need to *open our arms* and invite the Spirit to live within us. We need to pray: "I welcome you into my life, even when I feel weary, and into this moment right now to show me how to love as you do." Here's what Paul had to say about this kind of prayer:

Meanwhile, the moment we get tired in the waiting, God's Spirit is right alongside helping us along. If we don't know how or what to pray, it doesn't matter. He does our praying in and for us, making prayer out of our wordless sighs, our aching groans. He knows us far better than we know ourselves, knows our pregnant condition, and keeps us present before God.

3. We need to *open our hearts* to accept how the Spirit is counseling us. We need to pray: "Guide me even when I don't know what to say or do in this moment. I want to hear your truthful teaching even if it's tough to hear." Here's what Jesus said:

> "But when the Friend comes, the Spirit of the Truth, he will take you by the hand and guide you into all the truth there is."

4. We need to *open our mouths* to boldly ask for the Spirit's power within and through us. We need to pray: "Work wonders though me in this moment for this person I'm trying to love. Give me the power I don't have to love this person the way you do." Here's what Paul said about this:

> God can do anything, you know—far more than you could ever imagine or guess or request in your wildest dreams! He does it not by pushing us around but by working within us, his Spirit deeply and gently within us.

5. We need to *open ourselves* by giving our lives over to the Spirit each day. We need to pray: "I want to surrender my will to yours and depend on you to fill me with your desires and your

motivations in loving others. I am dependent on you for loving others at the highest levels. I can't do it without you." In writing to the Ephesians, Paul said:

> Now God has us where he wants us, with all the time in this world and the next to shower grace and kindness upon us in Christ Jesus. Saving is all his idea, and all his work. All we do is trust him enough to let him do it. It's God's gift from start to finish! We don't play the major role. If we did, we'd probably go around bragging that we'd done the whole thing! No, we neither make nor save ourselves. God does both the making and saving. He creates each of us by Christ Jesus to join him in the work he does, the good work he has gotten ready for us to do, work we had better be doing.

As I said, it's all about the leaning—as we open our eyes, arms, hearts, mouths, and selves. That's when the Spirit-filled life becomes real. That's when our Friend reminds us how to love like Jesus, prompting, guiding, and counseling us. If this idea of falling in step with the Holy Spirit is new to you or if you've heard this message your entire life but still want to incorporate the Spirit into your life at a more practical level, read the appendix of this book. I take a deeper dive into life in the Spirit and provide additional suggestions for you in the appendix: How to Make Loving Like That a Habit.

The Spirit produces Christ's character within us in ways we can't muster on our own. That's why Scripture even identifies "the fruit of the Spirit": love, joy, peace, patience, kindness, goodness, faithfulness, gentleness, and self-control. This isn't a to-do list we need to accomplish. We can't will our way into embodying these loving qualities consistently. Nope. We don't have to put ourselves through this unproductive and self-sabotaging exercise. We simply need to rely on his Spirit—our Friend—to produce these qualities through us. The more we lean into the Spirit of Christ to manifest these loving qualities in our relationships, the more evident they become.

But let me remind you of what I said at the outset in this book: this whole idea of loving like Jesus isn't rational. The bar he set for loving others seems completely out of reach. That's why we need to reason with our heart as much as our head if we are to fall in step with the Spirit of Christ in us. And, of course, this will make little to no rational sense to the person who hasn't yet invited God to live in them. Here's how Paul put it to the early Christians in Rome:

But if God himself has taken up residence in your life, you can hardly be thinking more of yourself than of him. Anyone, of course, who has not welcomed this invisible but clearly present God, the Spirit of Christ, won't know what we're talking about. But for you who welcome him, in whom he dwells—even though you still experience all the limitations of sin—you yourself experience life on God's terms. It stands to reason, doesn't it, that if the alive-and-present God who raised Jesus from the dead moves into your life, he'll do the same thing in you that he did in Jesus, bringing you alive to himself? When God lives and breathes in you (and he does, as surely as he did in Jesus), you are delivered from that dead life. With his Spirit living in you, your body will be as alive as Christ's!

Jesus knew this whole thing with the Holy Spirit was a bit of a head-scratcher, that the idea of the Spirit was not an easy concept to absorb. The Spirit's mystical nature causes our rational mind to immediately question how such an experience could be real. That's why he used a tangible word picture to explain it.

Jesus and the disciples had completed their memorable meal, celebrating Passover in the upper room—their last supper. They were leaving the house, walking through the streets out by the city gate, headed to the garden of Gethsemane on the lower slope of the Mount of Olives. It's not a long walk. In fact, I walked it myself to better imagine this moment. It's about a half mile from the wall of Jerusalem to Gethsemane. But it's hilly—across the Kidron Valley. And since the Sanhedrin, the supreme court of ancient Israel, was searching for Jesus, I'm sure Jesus and the disciples didn't linger. They walked at a fast pace, but Jesus used the time wisely. He knew it would be the last opportunity to teach these men he'd mentored for more than three years. Judas had already left to carry out his betrayal. The ominous timeline was set in motion. Jesus knew what awaited him in Gethsemane and how it would change everything forever.

So he gave this masterful lesson on the go:

> "Live in me. Make your home in me just as I do in you. In the same way that a branch can't bear grapes by itself but only by being joined to the vine, you can't bear fruit unless you are joined with me.
>
> I am the Vine, you are the branches. When you're joined with me and I with you, the relation intimate and organic, the harvest is sure to be abundant."

As Jesus painted this picture, the group would have been walking alongside vineyards that were all over the valley between the city and the garden. The master teacher, Jesus, knew this visual lesson would stick. He made it easy to understand and remember.

The branches get their energy and strength from the vine. They can't produce any fruit without being connected to the vine. And if we are to love like Jesus we need to stay connected to him. The more we abide in him and lean into his Spirit within us, the more fruit we bear—the more we love like Jesus.

Here's the bottom line: loving like Jesus isn't *achieved* as much as it is *received*. The instant I realize that I can't love at the highest levels without him loving through me, I receive what's needed. Like turning water into wine, God turns my best efforts, which too often fall short, into something better than I could have ever offered on my own.

That's how you love like Jesus.

HOW TO MAKE LOVING LIKE THAT A HABIT

Let's not just talk about love; let's practice real love. This is the only way we'll know we're living truly, living in God's reality.

—Jesus

You've probably heard the riddle about the five frogs sitting on a log. Four decide to jump off. How many are left? *One*, of course, you say. But the answer is five. Why? Because there's a difference between deciding and doing. It's one thing to be motivated for action and another to cultivate the discipline to actually do it. In other words, the real issue is to make loving like Jesus more than a decision. That's the start. But the key is to make it a habit.

More accurately, it's to make the five qualities I've outlined in this book—being mindful, approachable, grace-full, bold, and self-giving—a lifestyle pattern of behavior. And that begins by cultivating what experts call a *keystone habit*. What's that? It's the development of a habit that is so important it starts a chain effect in your life, producing numerous positive outcomes. A keystone habit comes with a trickle-down effect. Good results ripple through your life as a result of fostering a keystone habit.

"We are what we repeatedly do," said Aristotle. And modern-day social scientists couldn't agree more. Your life today is essentially the sum of your habits—for good or bad. How in shape or out of shape you are? A result of your habits. Your financial health? A result of your habits. How productive or unproductive you are? A result of your habits. Researchers at Duke University found that more than 40 percent of the actions we perform each day aren't actual decisions. They're habits.

What you repeatedly do, day to day, ultimately forms the kind of person you are—especially when it comes to loving others at the highest level. So, now that you've read the book, you can think of this appendix as your action plan to help you embody the principles you've studied. When paired with the deeper lessons from the book's chapters, this appendix is a practical guide for where to go next.

The Path of Least Resistance

I grew up in Boston, where city planning gravitates around the mentality of a seventeenth-century cow. Literally. The roads in Boston were actually formed by utilizing existing cow paths formed in the 1600s. Navigating the topography, cows moved wherever it was easiest to move, taking the smallest incline, for example. The more cows that passed through a certain area, the more clearly defined the path became. And eventually those paths became roads that crisscross and curl through the city to this very day.

How could this be? Because, unless you deliberately intervene, energy moves where it is easiest to go. This is true not only for cows but for all nature, whether it be water, wind, electrical currents, animals, or human beings. We naturally move along the path of least resistance. It's instinctual. It's a law. But here's another: *With a bit of intention and some discipline, you can reconfigure your personal path of least resistance, creating a new habit for your behavior, until it becomes automatic.* You can deliberately change an old habit or create a new one.

That's what Tony Dungy did. As a professional football coach, Tony wanted to get players to stop making so many decisions during a game and, instead, react automatically, habitually. If he could instill the right habits, he knew his team would win. "Champions don't do extraordinary things," he reasoned. "They follow the habits they've learned."

But Tony had a problem. Every time he interviewed for an NFL coaching position, his philosophy fell flat. Team owners weren't buying it. Well, they weren't buying it until the woeful Tampa Bay Buccaneers called in 1996 and asked Tony to be their head coach. Tony immediately put his strategy to work. He didn't focus on an elaborate playbook or having players memorize hundreds of formations. He simply had them learn a few key moves until they'd become second nature. He wanted to take decision-making out of the game for his players. He coached each player, individually, to understand the visual cues that would trigger habits. If the opposing guard stepped out of formation or the running back's foot indicated a pass, his players wouldn't have to think about what to do. They would respond out of habit—without giving it a thought. It took almost a year for Tony's habits to take hold. But when they did it was brilliant.

Tony's system of creating automatic thinking eventually turned the Bucs into one of the league's most successful teams. He became the only NFL coach in history to reach the playoffs in ten consecutive years, the first African American coach to win a Super Bowl, and one of the most respected figures in professional athletics. All because he understood the power of cultivating productive habits. So much so that he removed the need for decision-making and freed up his player's brains to act with greater efficiency and more intelligence.

And that's the point—freeing up our brains. Once a habit starts unfolding, the gray matter in our brain is free to quiet itself or chase other ideas. Consider something as simple as brushing your teeth. Before you start your day, you pick up your toothbrush and automatically put toothpaste on it. You do this without thinking. It's automatic. Habits like this free up your brain. They help it run more efficiently.

But conserving mental effort is tricky, because if our brains power down at the wrong moment, we might fail to notice something important. That's why our basal ganglia—the inner part of our brain that is associated with routine behaviors—have devised a clever system to determine when to let habits take over. They look for a cue or a hint (for example, a television commercial, a certain place, a time of day, a candy bar, an emotion, a person) and tell our brain to cede control to a particular habit. That's when the brain stops fully participating in decision-making. It stops working so hard. And if we learn to create new neurological routines, if we take control of a habit, we can force bad tendencies into the background and put a more productive habit into play, making it our new and personalized path of least resistance.

That's exactly what I want to help you do through this appendix. Why? I want to help you create a new neurological routine. I want you to train your basal ganglia to make it easier for you to love like Jesus. I want to help you make the behaviors we've talked about—being mindful, approachable, grace-full, bold, and self-giving—more automatic so that you don't have to burn up your brain making countless decisions to love like Jesus. Instead, love will be more and more a part of your relationships because you *don't* have to think about it. Love will become a habit. And it hinges on the secret Jesus gave us to love like he did.

Don't Forget Your Supernatural Friend

In the five chapters of this book, I have laid out a framework for understanding how we can love more like Jesus. I've done my best to not only pinpoint what

Jesus taught and modeled for us, but to highlight what too often keeps us from doing it and, more important, what we can do to embody love like this in our own lives. But even with our best efforts I confess that it becomes an impossibility to measure up to Jesus, the perfect image of God.

We can know what to do and even be willing to do it, but there is still the *doing*. And that's where we get hung up. We try, and we fail. We try again, and we fail. And we continue to fail until we internalize this truth: *we don't do the loving alone; the Holy Spirit helps us love others.* This isn't a clever way of turning the tables or letting us off the hook. It's how it works. It's truth. It's how we grow spiritually. It's what some Christian traditions call "spiritual formation"—when the Spirit forms us into people who love like Jesus. As I noted in the conclusion of this book, it all comes down to leaning into and falling in step with the Holy Spirit, our Friend.

The Spirit is not an afterthought or a tagalong. The Spirit was there at creation—from the beginning—and the Bible details a close relationship between Jesus and the Holy Spirit during his entire earthly life. Jesus was conceived by the Holy Spirit. The Holy Spirit descended on Jesus like a dove during his baptism in the Jordan River. Jesus performed his miracles through the power of the Spirit. At the Last Supper, Jesus promised to send the Holy Spirit to his disciples. When Jesus' closest earthly companions betrayed him and denied him, the Spirit walked with Jesus all the way to the cross, empowering him. And the Spirit was there on Easter Sunday to raise Jesus in power.

It is impossible to ignore the integral relationship of Jesus and the Holy Spirit. And it is this same Holy Spirit who walks with us today.

Of course, this mystical proposition can sound abstract, transcendent, metaphysical, and even bizarre to the rational mind. If you're riddled with questions, I understand. We can't see or quantify the Spirit, so how do we know anything about the Spirit? How do we receive God's Spirit? How do we know when the Spirit, the Helper, is in us, enabling us to love like Jesus? In fact, what is the Holy Spirit—or *who* is the Holy Spirit? Questions abound.

That's why I dedicate this appendix to the practical tactics for shaping our hearts and our habits to routinely walking with the Spirit, our Friend, so that we can come closer and closer to loving like Jesus. This is the single most important habit we can ever cultivate. It's our keystone habit—the one that positively impacts every relationship we have.

Let me say this clearly: if you get a lock on this habit of falling in step with the Holy Spirit, you don't have to make nearly as many decisions about being mindful, approachable, grace-full, bold, or self-giving. They will happen without much thought at all. The Spirit will help you, guide you, and comfort you all along the way as you learn to love more and more like Jesus. So how do you develop such a "love habit"? The answer is found in two time-tested methods: connect with the Spirit daily and get to know the Spirit's voice.

Connecting Daily with the Spirit

A famous first-century rabbi in Israel named Akiva was shepherding his flocks when he noticed a tiny stream trickling down a hillside and dripping onto a massive boulder. The rock bore a deep impression where the water had dripped over the centuries, hollowing away the stone. Akiva commented, "If mere water can do this to hard rock, how much more can God's Word carve a way into my heart of flesh?"

The slow but steady impact of each small droplet, year after year, completely reformed the stone. The same is true for you and me when we routinely become conscious of the Spirit in our lives, day after day. We can't cultivate a life-changing keystone habit overnight. It results from a daily intention, if only for a few minutes, of reflection and prayer. To live a

Spirit-filled life, we need to be conscious of the Spirit within us. We need to meditate on God's Word and say a prayer—even if we don't know what to pray. Scripture tells us that the Spirit prays for us when we are at a loss:

> The moment we get tired in the waiting, God's Spirit is right alongside helping us along. If we don't know how or what to pray, it doesn't matter. He does our praying in and for us, making prayer out of our wordless sighs, our aching groans. He knows us far better than we know ourselves, knows our pregnant condition, and keeps us present before God.

A simple quiet time of reading a passage of the Bible and saying a prayer—daily—is like the dripping water on a seemingly unchangeable stone. It gradually alters our lives. It slowly shapes our heart. Daily meditation brings God's Spirit into our consciousness and awakens our intuitive mind to hear that "still small voice."

Jesus recommended this practice himself:

> "Here's what I want you to do: Find a quiet, secluded place so you won't be tempted to role-play before God. Just be there as simply and honestly as you can manage. The focus will shift from you to God."

If you want to hear the heart of God, moments of quiet are essential. Life is loud. The noise of hustle and bustle fills every frequency in our day and it's easy—in fact, it's the path of least resistance—to become deaf to God's voice. Even when we are intent on listening, we too often get sidetracked. It takes very little to distract us from quieting our mind. "I neglect God and his angels, for the noise of a fly," said English poet John Donne. I so identify with this sentiment. As a psychologist, I know how to practice proactive listening with a patient. In a counseling session, I know how to turn on what Theodor Reik called "listening with a third ear." But to listen aggressively to the Spirit's quiet whispers throughout my day when so many noises clamor for my attention? That's a challenge. And I know it's nearly impossible if I haven't set aside at least a dedicated moment to breathe a prayer and be conscious of God speaking to me through his Word.

In my early years of being a God-follower, I didn't really get it. I thought a daily quiet time was an act of discipline—something to check off my to-do list— something to show God that I was devout. And it was often tough. In fact, I frequently failed. Why? Because I was missing the point. A quiet time becomes a dreaded discipline if you're not doing it to become conscious of God's voice. But once you see how your meditative moments help you hear the Spirit more clearly and more frequently, life changes. The Spirit's "still small voice" gets a little louder. Soon you can't imagine going a day without intentionally connecting with the Spirit. "Every time you listen with great attentiveness to the voice that calls you the Beloved," said noted author Henri Nouwen, "you will discover within yourself a desire to hear that voice longer and more deeply."

It's the daily repetition of a quiet time with God that bores an unfathomable impression on our hearts. A slow but steady stream of intentions to be more Spirit-conscious—day after day—reforms our soul, enabling us to love more and more like Jesus.

Getting to Know the Spirit's Voice

On a recent visit to Jerusalem, I wanted to take the fifteen-minute drive to Bethlehem. It's not as simple as the short distance between the two cities suggests. It requires a border crossing because Bethlehem is under Palestinian control. As I waited for the armed soldiers to check my passport, I witnessed a scene that Jesus almost certainly saw two thousand years ago: Bedouin shepherds bringing their flocks home from the various pastures they had grazed during the day.

I asked my Israeli guide about these modern-day shepherds and learned that the flocks end up at the same watering hole around dusk. They get all mixed up together, eight or nine small flocks turning into a convention of thirsty sheep. Their shepherds don't worry about the mix-up, however. When it's time to go home, each one issues his or her own distinctive call, a special whistle or a particular tune on a reed pipe, and then each shepherd's sheep withdraw from the crowd to follow their own shepherd home. They know their shepherd's voice, and it's the only one they follow.

It's another analogy to illustrate what happens with us when we become attuned to the Spirit's voice. Shepherds are mentioned dozens of times throughout the Bible—from Genesis to Revelation. Jesus referred to himself as "the good shepherd" and often used the qualities of a shepherd to teach important lessons: "I know my own sheep and my own sheep know me."

So how do we become more attuned to hearing the Spirit's voice like the sheep hear their shepherd? I believe the answer is found, in part, by clearing our head. You've got to have a clear head if you want to hear a clear voice from God. That is, you've got to relax the tension around your overthinking to make room for your intuition. The word *intuition* comes from the Latin word *intueri*, which is roughly translated as meaning "to contemplate." You see, our intuition stems from what we are considering, what we are sensitive to or attuned to. "The [voice] of the Spirit come[s] in the most extraordinarily gentle ways," says author Oswald Chambers, "and if you are not sensitive enough to detect his voice you will quench it." So, if you want to hear from God, you've got to slow down enough to clear your head and be attuned to his Spirit. That's when the sacred gift of God's whispers is heard—that's when you become accustomed to his voice.

I can almost hear you asking: "How in the world can I be still when life is so fast?" It's a fair question. God does not expect us to be contemplative monks to hear his voice. He merely asks that we be attuned to his presence—even in the calamity and chaos of our lives. Being still does not always mean retreating to a quiet place. It means quieting our mind, even during chaos, by not trying to figure everything out. It means not striving so hard. It means putting your mind at ease and letting God be God. It means being conscious of the Spirit and seeing the big picture.

"We may ignore, but we can nowhere evade, the presence of God," said C. S. Lewis. "The world is crowded with Him. He walks everywhere incognito." Lewis, of course, did not mean that it's a game of trying to figure out where God is. Quite the contrary. God is everywhere, even in the most common of places, when we quiet our minds enough to notice. You see, the complexity of our rational mind, so often troubled with deadlines, worries, tasks, and drives, keeps us looking down. It forces us to focus, almost exclusively, on our own story. It prevents us from looking up to see the bigger story. And the bigger story, the story of all stories, is that God is God.

You've probably heard the contemporary adage: "There is a God, and it's not me." Sometimes that may be the only prayer we need to become more attuned to the Spirit's voice.

"A journey begins with a single step." As clichés go, that's pretty wise. After all, walking in the footsteps of Jesus, loving others like him, is incredibly audacious. Right? It's so lofty we can fear taking the first step. That's why I want to conclude this appendix by making a simple but crucial point: loving like Jesus requires a "leap of faith." No doubt about it. It requires us to reason with our heart as much as with our head. And it merely asks that you take the first step. Martin Luther King Jr. may have said it best: "Take the first step in faith. You don't have to see the whole staircase, just take the first step."

When it comes to your relationships, I'm praying that you take a leap of faith and fall in step with the Spirit this very day.

ACKNOWLEDGMENTS

I'm so honored to be surround by incredible people who have influenced the message of this book. For starters, the team at Thomas Nelson has put a refreshing breeze into my publishing sails. I can't say thanks enough to Brian Hampton, Webster Younce, Joey Paul, Jenny Baumgartner, Brigitta Nortker, Stephanie Tresner, and Tiffany Sawyer. And a special thanks for my longtime friend and agent, Sealy Yates, for bringing me to Thomas Nelson (everything you said about this relationship is true).

Keenly Interactive that includes Jason Lehman, Todd Flaming, Jamie Mitchell, Steve Richardson, Melinda Lehman, Becca Holt and Bob Lehman is savvy and passionate. They are taking the message of this book higher than I ever could. Steve and Barbara Uhlmann may not even know it, but this book wouldn't even exist without their unflinching support.

ACKNOWLEDGMENTS

Lysa TerKeurst, you were an amazing guide for my family and me as we walked through Jerusalem and beyond to follow the footsteps of Jesus. To have you review this manuscript with me in it's first draft was truly the extra mile. Thanks also to Ron and Katie Robertson and Jim and Joy Zorn. Many of the ideas in these pages were explored with you while sailing through the San Juans together. Our late-night talks, as well as your abiding friendship are an inspiration to me.

I'm also deeply appreciative of Brian Mosley and his team at RightNow. We've traveled a long path together and it's always a genuine delight. Ashton Owens is my go-to graphics guy that helps me in countless ways with his winsome personality and incredible exper-tise. Ranjy Thomas, I don't know how I could have a stronger and more enthusiastic encourager than you.

My Loveology team is simply incredible. A heartfelt thanks to Ryan Farmer, Halie Simonds, Darin Ault, David Kinney, Jenee Crowther, and Michael Gibson. Same is true of my 5% Club—you know who you are.

Finally, I want to once again thank Leslie and our boys for all the untold hours we sacrificed as I wrote "into the wee hours." I don't know how a writer, a husband, or a dad, could ask for anything more. To all of you, thank you a million times over.

ABOUT THE AUTHOR

Les Parrott, PhD, is a psychologist and #1 *New York Times* bestselling author. He and his wife, Dr. Leslie Parrott, are cofounders of the game-changing Deep Love Assessment (see DeepLove.com). Dr. Parrott's books have sold over three million copies in more than two dozen languages and include the award-winning *Saving Your Marriage Before It Starts*. Dr. Parrott has been featured in *USA Today* and the *New York Times*. He's appeared on CNN, Fox News, *Good Morning America*, *The Today Show*, *The View*, and *Oprah*. Visit LesAndLeslie.com.

NOTES

INTRODUCTION

xvi "the most excellent way": 1 Corinthians 12:31 NIV.

xvii "The mind is its own place": John Milton, *Paradise Lost*, bk. 1, lines 254–255.

xvii "For as he thinks": Proverbs 23:7 NKJV.

xviii "Christian thinking is": Oswald Chambers, *Christian Disciplines*, vol. 1, *The Discipline of Divine Guidance*, quoted in "Thinking," *The Quotable Oswald Chambers*, ed. David McCasland (Grand Rapids: Discovery House, 2011), e-book edition.

xix "But eyes are blind": Antoine de Saint-Exupéry, *The Little Prince*, trans. Richard Howard (Boston: Houghton Mifflin Harcourt, 2000), 71.

xx The moment we open: 2 Timothy 1:7.

xx "You'll be changed": Romans 12:2.

xxiv He went on to say: Martin E. P. Seligman, "Positive
Feeling and Positive Character," chap. 1 in *Authentic
Happiness* (New York: Simon & Schuster, 2002), 90.

xxvii "Once I had brains": L. Frank Baum, *The Wonderful
Wizard of Oz* (Chicago: George M. Hill, 1900), 58,
accessed at Archive.org, https://archive.org/details
/wond_wiz_oz.

CHAPTER 1: MINDFUL

2 "invisible gorilla" test: Dan J. Simons and Christopher F.
Chabris, "Gorillas in Our Midst: Sustained Inattentional
Blindness for Dynamic Events," *Perception* 28, no. 9
(1999): 1059–74.

2 The study has been replicated: Steven B. Most et. al,
"How Not to Be Seen: The Contribution of Similarity and
Selective Ignoring to Sustained Inattentional Blindness,"
Psychological Science 12, no. 1 (January 2001), 9–17.

4 Using eye-tracking technology: Trafton Drew, Melissa
L.-H. Võ, and Jeremy M. Wolfe, "The Invisible Gorilla
Strikes Again: Sustained Inattentional Blindness in
Expert Observers," *Psychological Science* 24, no. 9
(September 2013): 1848–53.

16 "A man was going down": Luke 10:30 ESV.

18 "It is hard to think": John Darley and C. Daniel Batson,
"From Jerusalem to Jericho: A Study of Situational and
Dispositional Variables in Helping Behavior," *Journal
of Personality and Social Psychology* 27, no. 1 (1973):
100–08.

19 "transformed by the renewing": Romans 12:2 NKJV.

21 "New dendrites are formed": Andrew Newberg
and Mark Robert Waldman, *How God Changes*

Your Brain: Breakthrough Findings from a Leading Neuroscientist (New York: Ballantine Books, 2010), 3.

21   "Whoever belongs to God": John 8:47 NIV.

21   "Whoever is united": 1 Corinthians 6:17 NIV.

22   And when it's just pastors: Audrey Barrick, "Survey: Christians Worldwide Too Busy for God," Christian Post, July 30, 2007, www.christianpost.com/news /survey-christians-worldwide-too-busy-for-god-28677/.

22   "Be still": Psalm 46:10 NKJV.

22   "We may ignore": C. S. Lewis, *Letters to Malcolm: Chiefly on Prayer* (London: Geoffrey Bles, 1964; Project Gutenberg, 2016), letter 14, https://gutenberg.ca/ebooks /lewiscs-letterstomalcolm/lewiscs-letterstomalcolm-00-h .html#chapter14.

23   "Earth's crammed with heaven": Elizabeth Barrett Browning, *Aurora Leigh* (London: Chapman and Hall, 1857), 304, accessed at Archive.org, https://archive.org /details/auroraleigh00browrich.

23   "If any of you lacks": James 1:5 NIV.

24   "to see": *Online Etymology Dictionary*, s.v. "weid," accessed January 15, 2018, https://www.etymonline.com /word/*weid-.

24   "clear": *HELPS Word Studies*, s.v. "sophía," BibleHub .com, http://biblehub.com/greek/4678.htm.

CHAPTER 2: APPROACHABLE

28   simple strategy called Cyberball: Kipling D. Williams and Lisa Zadro, "Ostracism: On Being Ignored, Excluded, and Rejected," in *Interpersonal Rejection*, ed. Mark R. Leary (New York: Oxford University Press, 2001), 21–53.

28   same two regions: Kipling D. Williams and Steve A. Nida, "Ostracism: Consequences and Coping," *Current Directions in Psychological Science* 20, no. 2 (April 2011): 71.

31   75 percent of all participants: Solomon E. Asch, "Opinions and Social Pressure (1955)," in *Readings About the Social Animal*, eds. Joshua Aronson and Elliot Aronson, 11th ed. (New York: Worth, 2011), 17–26, Kindle edition.

36   "Your faith has saved you": Luke 7:36–50.

37   "Let the little children": Matthew 19:14 ESV.

40   "Please accept my resignation": Groucho Marx, *Groucho and Me* (1959; Cambridge, MA: Da Capo Press, 1995), 320.

40   "Because, Michelis": Nikos Kazantzakis, *Christ Recrucified* (Oxford, Bruno Cassirer, 1966), 186–87.

41   "A man is never so proud": C. S. Lewis, "Christianity and Culture" in *Christian Reflections* (Grand Rapids, Eerdmans, 2014), 16.

42   "Two men went up to the Temple": Luke 18:11–14.

45   Rembrandt isn't the only: Luke 15; the story was infinitely more about the father's love than the prodigal's misconduct.

45   "the crown and flower": William R. Nicoll, "Lost and Found," in *Expositor's Bible Commentary*, chap. 21, commentary on Luke 15, accessed at StudyLight.com, https://www.studylight.org/commentaries/teb/luke-15.html.

46   "This man receives sinners": Luke 15:2 ESV.

46   "When he was still a long": Luke 15:20.

48   "You are now cut off": Kenneth E. Bailey, *The Cross & the Prodigal*, 2nd ed. (Downers Grove, IL: InterVarsity Press, 2005), 52.

49 "not to be served": Mark 10:45 ESV.

49 "Each of you should be concerned": Philippians 2:4 NET.

50 "I tell you, love your enemies": Matthew 5:44 WEB.

50 "If someone slaps you": Luke 6:28–30.

51 "gives his best": Matthew 5:45–47.

51 "Prayer doesn't change God": Matthew 7:12.

55 "Give without expecting a return": Luke 6:35–36.

CHAPTER 3: GRACE-FULL

60 "Mercy gave the Prodigal Son": Max Lucado (@MaxLucado), Twitter post, January 17, 2011, 7:19 a.m., https://twitter.com/maxlucado/status/2702230035628 4416?lang=en.

60 "Laughter is the closest thing": Quoted in Robert J. Fitzhenry, *The Harper Book of Quotations*, 3rd ed. (New York: Collins Reference, 2005), 223.

61 Jesus modeled it time and again: John 8:2–11.

63 "Christ accepts us as we are": Walter Trobisch, *Love Yourself* (Downers Grove, IL: InterVarsity Press, 1976), 26.

63 "Jesus did not identify the person": Thielicke, *How the World Began*, 62.

66 "Don't worry, I will": Paraphrased from Luke 23:34–43.

69 "incompetent people don't know": Justin Kruger and David Dunning, "Unskilled and Unaware of It: How Difficulties in Recognizing One's Own Incompetence Can Lead to Inflated Self-Assessments," *Journal of Personality and Social Psychology* 77, no. 6 (1999): 1121–34.

70 *negativity bias*: Carey K. Morewedge, "Negativity Bias in Attribution of External Agency," *Journal of Experimental Psychology: General* 138, no. 4 (2009): 535–45.

70 "We *need* other people's faults": Terry D. Cooper,

Making Judgments Without Being Judgmental (Downers Grove, IL: IVP Books, 2006), 23.

70 "Do not judge": Matthew 7:1 NIV.

71 "Rare is the person": Lars Wihelmsson, *Vital Christianity* (Torrance, CA: Martin Press, 1982), 60.

74 "I will never disown you": Matthew 26:35 NIV.

74 "We left everything": Matthew 19:27.

76 "Friend, I haven't been unfair": Matthew 20:8–15.

77 In another parable, Jesus: Matthew 13:24–30.

78 "Don't pick on people": Matthew 7:1–5.

82 "Whoever has been forgiven": Luke 7:47 NIV.

82 "To be a Christian means": C. S. Lewis, *The Weight of Glory* (New York: HarperOne, 2001), 183.

83 "I distinctly remember": William Eleazar Barton, *The Life of Clara Barton: Founder of the American Red Cross*, vol. 2 (Boston: Houghton Mifflin, 1922), 345.

83 "Curiosity, has its own reason": Einstein to William Miller in *Life* magazine, quoted in Alice Calaprice, ed., *The Ultimate Quotable Einstein* (Princeton: Princeton University Press, 2011), 425.

86 "To be as accident-prone": Rabbi Shlomo Carlebach in conversation with Bo Lozoff in Lozoff's book *It's a Meaningful Life: It Just Takes Practice* (New York: Penguin, 2001), chapter 1, e-book edition.

CHAPTER 4: BOLD

90 *pluralistic ignorance*: H. J. O'Gorman, "The Discovery of Pluralistic Ignorance: An Ironic Lesson," *Journal of the History of the Behavioral Sciences* 22, no. 4 (1986): 333–47.

94 "You strain out a gnat": Matthew 23:24 TLB.

95 "You religion scholars and Pharisees": Matthew 23:23–24.

95 "You Pharisees clean the outside": Luke 11:39 NIV.

96 "When you do something": Matthew 6:2–6.

99 they know he is one of them: Matthew 21:12–14.

100 Jesus corrected his wrong motives: Matthew 8:18–22.

100 "You should be more like": Luke 10:38–42.

104 "There's trouble ahead": Luke 6:26.

105 "Everything is usually so masked": Anne Lamott, *Traveling Mercies: Some Thoughts on Faith* (New York: Anchor Books, 2000), 215.

110 "If a fellow believer hurts": Matthew 18:15.

110 "If you enter your place of worship": Matthew 5:23–24.

110 "Don't lose a minute" Matthew 5:25.

110 "Confront him with the need": Matthew 18:17.

111 "Faithful are the wounds": Proverbs 27:6 AMP.

111 "Don't say anything you don't mean": Matthew 5:33–37.

111 a man named Nathanael: John 1:43–51 NRSV.

111 "Here is truly an Israelite": John 1:47 NRSV.

112 "Real isn't how you are made": Margery Williams, *The Velveteen Rabbit* (Garden City, NY: Doubleday, 1922; Project Gutenberg, 2004), http://www.gutenberg.org /files/11757/11757-h/11757-h.htm.

113 "And he understood that sawdust": Ibid.

115 "To love at all is to be vulnerable": C. S. Lewis, *The Four Loves* (New York: Harcourt Brace, 1991), 121.

116 the group Jesus most often criticized: Matthew 22:15–22.

116 "making one's own wounds": Henri Nouwen, *The Wounded Healer: Ministry in Contemporary Society* (1972; New York: Doubleday, 1979), 88.

118 "Confront him with the need" Matthew 18:17.

CHAPTER 5: SELF-GIVING

120 "I'm O.K., You're Selfish": Andrew J. Cherlin, "I'm O.K., You're Selfish," *New York Times Magazine*, 1999, https://partners.nytimes.com/library/magazine /millennium/m5/poll-cherlin.html.

121 when you lose your life: Matthew 10:39 NIV

122 "Selfish people are, by definition": Bernard Rimland, "The Altruism Paradox," *Psychological Reports* 51, no. 2 (1982): 521–22, http://dx.doi.org/10.2466/pr0 .1982.51.2.521.

122 "Whoever finds his life": Matthew 10:39 NIV.

123 "hot spots": David Clewett et. al, "Noradrenergic Mechanisms of Arousal's Bidirectional Effects on Episodic Memory," *Neurobiology of Learning and Memory* 137 (2017): 1–14.

125 "Do this in remembrance": Luke 22:19 NIV.

126 "sons of thunder": Mark 3:16–17.

127 "The Son of Man": Matthew 20:28 NIV.

129 their final dinner together: Luke 22:24–30.

131 Please see comment for more information.

131 Researchers asked people in rural: Juan Camilo Cardenas, John Stranlund, and Cleve Willis, "Local Environmental Control and Institutional Crowding-Out," *World Development* 28, no. 10 (2000): 1719–33.

138 "Ask yourself what you want": Matthew 7:12.

138 "Do to others as you": Luke 6:31 NIV.

138 "Love your neighbor": Matthew 22:39 NKJV.

139 "What you do not want": Confucius, *Analects* 15:23, see comment for more information.

139 "This is the sum of duty": *Mahabharata* 5:1517.

139 "Hurt not others in ways": *Udānavarga* 5:18.

142 "To live happily is": *The Meditations of Marcus Aurelius Antonius the Roman Emperor*, trans. Meric Casaubon (London: A. and John Churchill; Sam. Smith and Tho. Bennet, 1692), bk. 11, sec. 15.

143 we can give our body: 1 Corinthians 13:3.

143 "Second fiddle": James S. Hewett, ed., *Illustrations Unlimited* (Wheaton, IL: Tyndale, 1988), 450.

144 "Love from the center": Romans 12:9–10.

CONCLUSION

149 "If anyone boasts": 1 John 4:20.

152 "We know truth": Blaise Pascal, *Pascal's Pensées* (1670; New York: Dutton, 1958), 258.

152 Christ lives in you: 1 John 4:15.

153 "I tried keeping rules": Galatians 2:19–21.

153 "This mystery has been": Colossians 1:27.

153 "You'll be changed": Romans 12:2.

154 "But when the Friend comes": John 16:13.

154 developed a structure of friendship: Phillip Moeller, "Why Good Friends Make You Happy," *Huffington Post*, March 15, 2012, https://www.huffingtonpost.com /2012/03/15/friendship-happiness_n_1348648.html.

155 "friendships based on character": Richard Kraut, "Aristotle's Ethics," in *Stanford Encyclopedia of Philosophy*, ed. Edward N. Zalta, Stanford University, article published May 1, 2001, revised April 21, 2014, https://plato.stanford.edu/entries/aristotle-ethics/.

155 And that's what Jesus is saying: John 14:16; 15:26; 16:7.

156 "Spirit of Knowledge": Isaiah 11:2 NKJV.

156 "Spirit of Comfort": John 14:16 AMP.

156 "Spirit of Grace": Hebrews 10:29 NIV.

156 "Spirit of Might": Isaiah 11:2 NIV.

156 "Spirit of God": 1 Corinthians 2:11 ESV.

159 "They ended up doing": Antoine Bechara, "Decision Making, Impulse Control and Loss of Willpower to Resist Drugs: A Neurocognitive Perspective," *Nature Neuroscience* 8, no. 11 (2005): 1458–63.

160 "transformed by the renewing": Romans 12:2 NIV.

160 "Let us keep in step": Galatians 5:25 NIV.

161 "Since this is the kind of life": Galatians 5:25–26.

162 "If you love me": John 14:17.

162 "Meanwhile, the moment we": Romans 8:26–27.

163 "But when the Friend": John 16:13.

163 "God can do anything": Ephesians 3:20.

164 "Now God has us where": Ephesians 2:8–10.

165 "the fruit of the Spirit": Galatians 5:22–23.

166 "But if God himself has": Romans 8:9–11.

167 "Live in me": John 15:4–5.

APPENDIX

170 "keystone habit": Charles Duhigg, *The Power of Habit: Why We Do What We Do in Life and Business* (New York: Random House, 2012).

170 40 percent of the actions: Bas Verplanken and Wendy Wood, "Interventions to Break and Create Consumer Habits," *Journal of Public Policy and Marketing* 25, no. 1 (2006): 90–103; See also David T. Neal, Wendy Wood, and Jeffrey M. Quinn, "Habits—A Repeat Performance," *Current Directions in Psychological Science* 15, no. 4 (2006): 198–202.

175 The Spirit was there at creation: Genesis 1:2.

175 Jesus was conceived: Luke 1:35.

175　on Jesus like a dove: Luke 3:22.

175　Jesus performed his miracles: Luke 4:14–19.

176　Jesus promised to send: John 14:26.

176　When Jesus' closest earthly: Hebrews 9:14.

176　And the Spirit was there: Romans 1:4.

176　enabling us to love: John 14:26 ESV.

177　"If mere water can do": Lois Tverberg, *Walking in the Dust of Rabbi Jesus* (Grand Rapids: Zondervan, 2012), 152.

178　"The moment we get tired" Romans 8:26–28.

178　"Here's what I want you": Matthew 6:6.

179　"I neglect God and": John Donne, *The Works of John Donne: Sermons. Devotions upon Emergent Occasions*, vol. 3 (London: John W. Parker, 1839), sermon LXXX, 477.

179　"listening with a third ear": Theodor Reik, *Listening with the Third Ear: The Inner Experience of a Psychoanalyst* (New York: Grove Press, 1956).

180　intentionally connecting with the Spirit: Mark Batterson, *Whisper: How to Hear the Voice of God* (New York: Crown Publishing, 2017).

180　"Every time you listen with great attentiveness": Henri J. M. Nouwen, *Life of the Beloved: Spiritual Living in a Secular World* (New York: Crossroad Publishing, 2002), 37.

181　Shepherds are mentioned dozens: Genesis 4:2; Rev. 12:5.

181　"I know my own sheep": John 10:14.

182　"The [voice] of the Spirit come[s]": Oswald Chambers, *My Utmost for His Highest: The Classic Daily Devotional* (1940; Uhrichsville, Ohio: Barbour Books, 2015), entry for August 13.

182 "We may ignore": C. S. Lewis, *Letters to Malcolm: Chiefly on Prayer* (San Diego: Harvest, 1964).

183 "Take the first step": Quoted by Marian Wright Edelman in "Kids First!" *Mother Jones*, May– June 1991, 77.

WHAT'S NEXT?

LOVE
LIKE THAT
5 Relationship Secrets from Jesus

A Companion Workbook
for Individuals and Small Groups

6 WEEK STUDY

Continue your journey to *Love Like That* with a
personal application workbook, chock-full of practical
exercises. It's ideal for personal study or as a six-week
group study that includes compelling video sessions.

LoveLikeThatBook.com

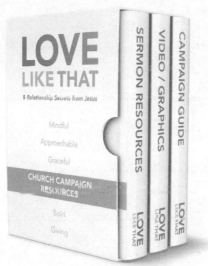

MAKE YOUR RELATIONSHIP

EVERYTHING YOU WANT IT TO BE.

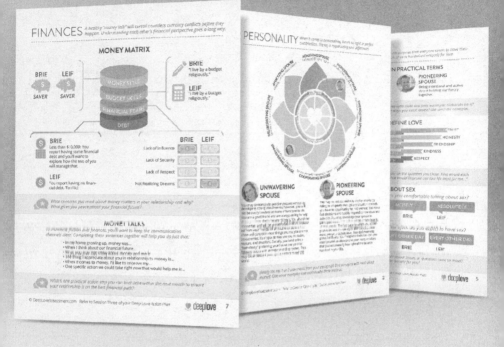

You won't find a more personalized and powerful relationship assessment than DEEP LOVE.

Each of the four sections of the report is essential to deepening the relationship with lasting, positive results:

1. **Personality**—because it's the best way to enhance empathy
2. **Communication**—because it's the lifeblood of love
3. **Conflict**—because every couple has friction
4. **Adaptability**—because even good relationships bump into bad things

TAKE THE ASSESSMENT AT **DEEPLOVE.COM**.